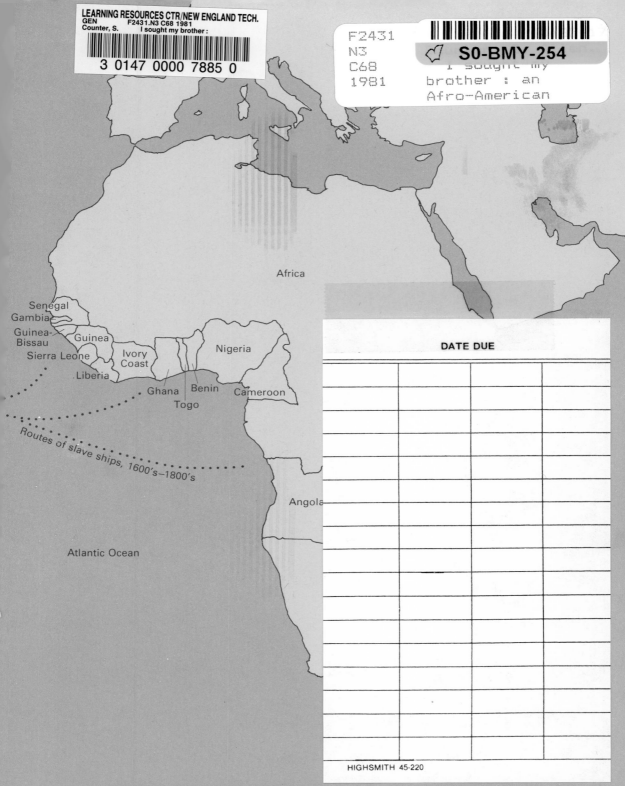

Africa

Senegal
Gambia
Guinea-
Bissau   Guinea
Sierra Leone   Ivory
Coast   Nigeria
Liberia
Ghana   Benin   Cameroon
Togo

Routes of slave ships, 1600's–1800's

Angola

Atlantic Ocean

NEW ENGLAND INSTITUTE
OF TECHNOLOGY
LEARNING RESOURCES CENTER

I Sought My Brother

The MIT Press
Cambridge, Massachusetts
London, England

I Sought My Brother

An Afro-American Reunion

S. Allen Counter and David L. Evans

We have changed the names of many persons and places in this
book to protect the privacy of our friends among the Bush Afro-
Americans.

This book was set in VIP Univers by DEKR Corporation and printed
by Halliday Lithograph and Nimrod Press and bound by Halliday
Lithograph in the United States of America.

The publication of this book has been assisted by grants from the
Rowland Foundation, Inc., and Randolph P. Compton.

Library of Congress Cataloging in Publication Data

Counter, S. Allen.
  I sought my brother.
  1. Djuka tribe. I. Evans, David L. II. Title.
F2431.N3C68   973'.0496   81-8419
ISBN 0-262-03079-9   AACR2

To Dabuwan: father, the good one

Contents

The Reunion   18

Epilogue   271

Foreword Alex Haley

My writing of *Roots* was preceded by long and painstaking research to learn as much as I could about the day-to-day living patterns of the people of representative eighteenth-century small West African villages. Only then was I able to feel at least reasonably equipped to project with any accuracy the infancy and then boyhood and the youth of Kunta Kinte, the principal person of *Roots*. And quick memories of that effort were stirred when I first heard about a pair of black scholars from Harvard University—S. Allen Counter, a neurobiologist, and David L. Evans, an electrical engineer—who had traveled deep into a jungle expanse of Surinam, South America, where few other outsiders had ever been. I heard with a thrill that they had visited the villages of a black bush people representing some three centuries of unmixed African descent—a bush people who had retained their ancestral African culture to such a dramatic degree that an equal could not easily be found today even in Africa itself.

Soon after I met Counter and Evans. They shared with me their wealth of photographs and their experiences, and a friendship was born that has not seen us very long out of touch.

It was while browsing one weekend in Harvard's rare books library that Counter and Evans had chanced upon the memoirs of the 1700s adventurer and illustrator John Gabriel Stedman. In his words and etchings, Stedman described both his interview findings and his own eyewitness accounts of how in the early 1600s numerous Africans arriving in Surinam on slave ships managed immediate violent escapes before they could be sold, and they fled into the nearest jungles, where they battled off the successive Dutch Army expeditions sent to capture them. Other Africans already enslaved heard of the valiant fighters and also escaped to join them, until the rebellious blacks had the physical forces to begin raiding plantations for food, arms, and yet more members, including their own black women. The acutely embarrassed and beleaguered Dutch military retaliated with every imaginable savagery, and Stedman in his memoirs told and pictured the horrible carnage among both the Dutch and the blacks.

Reading of this over two centuries later—after the black guerrillas had battled for generations, until their legal freedom to stay independent in the bush was finally granted—Counter and Evans were seized with what swiftly amounted to an obsession that a prime objective for Afro-American research would be to find out what had happened to those bush people.

Their determined efforts to translate their idea into action raised no few eyebrows among the number of Harvard friends and co-workers who lent them cooperative assistance. Soon, in the capital city of Paramaribo, Surinam's president and several government ministers provided the two black Americans with a plane, a pilot, and an interpreter-guide—along with strict cautions that the bush natives must be given every respectful deference and that only their leaders could grant outsiders entry into their villages.

The next phase of the adventure moved Counter and Evans to their first self-interrogation: Was their idea really as wise as it had seemed? As extremely nervous passengers in dugout canoes, they went skimming through treacherous rapids, watching the thick boulders against which obviously any collision would immerse all hands into waters abounding with man-eating piranha—not to mention their near panic each time the dugouts passed under over-hanging jungle vines and foliage from which large snakes could fall into the dugouts.

But an even more discomfiting psychic shock awaited their arrival at the first bush village. When the interpreter called out to the shoreline's crowded loinclothed bush people that the strangers were "Africans from a place called America," the bush people's spokesman demanded, "Well, if you are African, why are you wear-ing the clothes of the *bakrah* (white man)? . . . And are you still white man's slaves?" Counter and Evans were stunned beyond words. "Well, are you fighting? Or have you won your fight?" Counter and Evans managed a response that the black Americans' fight was still being fought.

I think I would do this book and its authors a disservice to at-tempt any condensing of what awaits readers in the pages that fol-low. I feel, in fact, that the more one reads, the more clearly one understands why Counter and Evans say that "neither of us could have realized just how the next few hundred miles and few days would change our thinking, our reactions, and indeed our entire lives."

Their text and photographs graphically tell and show how they visited among people and villages "like a timewarp . . . as if we had pressed a button for the Africa of the sixteenth and the seventeenth centuries." It will come as no surprise that, following their deeply moving first visit among the Surinam jungle's bush people, the Harvard pair returned many times.

In my opinion, this work of Counter and Evans has two principal and most timely significances. One is that recent years have seen an intensifiying of black petitioning that Afro-American history must

Foreword

become increasingly recognized both academically and among the general public. So it seems to me to follow that black scholars should undertake as a priority to lead in the varieties of field research that are sorely necessary to strengthen the corpus of the materials that document black history. There are scores of areas that offer, even guarantee, rich findings for diligent researchers—who will be not only inspired but challenged by this book.

Second, after a 300-year vigil defending and protecting their ancestral cultures and their independence, now, finally, inevitably, the Surinam bush people are facing what nearly always happens when the passage of time brings the trappings of technology with its attendant cultural erosion. For in the last section of this book, sadly, Counter and Evans tell how more and more of the younger men of the bush villages have begun to leave to take up work in nearby mining camps or other industries or in the cities—and fewer and fewer of them are returning to their native villages. What that portends for the bush culture is clear; it is only a matter of time. So this book chronicles the last days of the purity of what has been for three centuries one of the world's most unusual cultural enclaves.

Alex Haley

Preface

In 1964 I started to study the people of African origin who were scattered throughout North and South America. My primary interest was in analyzing their common lineage and in identifying the African traditions and characteristics they had preserved. At that time, the literary, social, and political interests of blacks in this country were focused on Africa and not on the Africanisms preserved in the so-called new world.

Today between Canada and lower Argentina there are over 50 million Afro-Americans, most of them descended from Africans who were forcibly taken from their native land by European adventurers and brought to this hemisphere to labor. I found that in the United States, blacks and whites alike had amazingly little knowledge of the prevalence or cultural backgrounds of the African-descended people in other countries of this hemisphere. In my travels throughout South America I found that the Afro-Americans of Colombia, Brazil, French Guiana, Surinam, and other countries had preserved many more African customs and linguistic features than had the Afro-Americans of the United States. In Brazil, for example, I witnessed Macumba (or so-called black magic) ceremonies in which people spoke in certain African tongues and worshipped African deities. In other South American and Caribbean countries I found African words in the language, African songs and dances, African foods, and herbal medical practices that could be traced directly back to Africa.

In the United States, with the exception of the South Carolina Sea Islands, almost every vestige of Africanism has been erased from the Afro-American culture. I cannot recall ever meeting an older black American who had any knowledge of African languages or specific African customs. That so much more has been preserved by our fellow Afro-Americans in the southern part of this hemisphere intrigued me. I drew a curve symbolizing the retention of African cultures and customs among Afro-Americans, and the curve showed a steady rise as one moved from the United States to the Caribbean, reaching a peak in certain parts of South America.

In addition to my primary interest, I was also searching for evidence of successful struggle against slavery. It is generally accepted that where antislavery activity was successful, the African culture remained at least partially intact. There is very little historical evidence of successful struggles against slavery in North America, however, and even those instances of armed struggle regarded as victorious were in reality only temporary successes. Great Afro-American freedom fighters like Nat Turner and Denmark Vessey had a profound social impact on the American society of that period, but their resistance movements were crushed before they really got off the ground and their names never appeared in the pages of most history books.

Like many other Afro-Americans, I have been told about the history of U.S. slavery since my childhood. Everyone spoke of the brutality of the enslavers, the inhuman working conditions, and the deaths of so many people of color from the beast-of-burden work loads. As I grew older, I was informed by the history books and stories I read that millions of "childlike" and "uncivilized" blacks were brought to these American shores by benevolent Europeans who had delivered them from certain pagan damnation in the jungle. Moreover, the early slaves were portrayed even by my school textbooks (when they were mentioned at all) as a docile people incapable of putting up any intellectual or physical resistance to slavery. I can remember wondering if there had been any black slaves, anywhere, who raised themselves to the dignity of armed struggle against their European enslavers. Did anyone, man or woman, put up a fight or raise a voice against slavery? My grandparents and great-grandmother told me of instances in history when a few southern blacks struggled against their enslavers for freedom. However, these historical moments were so rare and poorly recorded that even they could not remember details, dates, or times or any other critical facts. My great-grandmother would always respond by saying, "Freedom to do what? To go where? Even if they were set free there was nowhere to go. The only way we could have been free was to leave the United States entirely."

In high school I learned from one of those rare black teachers who had a sense of pride in Afro-American history that there were several large-scale antislavery rebellions by black freedom fighters in the Caribbean and a few in the United States. When I read about them in high school and college, I felt a strong identification with their struggles and a great admiration for their bravery. However, I was never thoroughly satisfied by the record of their efforts. Could their revolts really be called successful? Or were they only momentary expressions of rage and reactions to the brutal and inhuman system of slavery? It seemed to me that all other people of color who had resisted enslavement had something to show for it. The Indians (native Americans), for example, had peace treaties which Euro-Americans had petitioned *them* for in order to stop the successful Indian resistance to their armed invasions.

Preface

Through reading, I learned that the truly successful slave rebellions had occurred in the Caribbean and in South America, along with the preservation of African genetics, culture, and thought, and I decided to explore aspects of these cultures by visiting several Caribbean and South American countries.

In 1970 I joined the faculty of Harvard University and began teaching in the biological sciences. Although my primary research interest was in neurobiology, I continued to pursue my studies in Afro-American ethnography. To this end I made special efforts to avail myself of Harvard's vast library resources, including its outstanding rare book libraries. It was here that I began a more detailed investigation of the cultural and historical features of groups in South America and the Caribbean. My interest in these ethnographic studies was further enhanced by my scientific readings in the neurobiological literature, which made occasional references to "negro plant medicines" and other aspects of ethnopharmacology.

Steeping myself in the preemancipation and contemporary literature on these cultures, I decided to choose one country and culture to investigate. I wanted to visit and concentrate my studies on the country with the "purest" African-descended people in this hemisphere, and this was difficult to determine. Most of the literature on slavery or Afro-Americans in general was written by Euro-American anthropologists, historians, and other academics, and I found it difficult to trust their judgment or accuracy. I was scientifically, intellectually, and emotionally committed to this search and needed to make a decision on the basis of my own personal experience.

I visited Argentina in 1971 with the hope of working my way back north to Venezuela. In Argentina I found very few Afro-Americans and very little in the way of Afro-American culture, even though at one time in Argentina's history there were large numbers of African-descended people in the country.

The African presence in Brazil, a former Portuguese colony, is evident all over the country, particularly in the northeast. Portugal, a European country smaller than the state of Florida, enslaved millions of African citizens and brought them into Brazil and other parts of the Americas for over half a millennium. The Portuguese lead the list of European societies that brought death, destruction, and genocide to entire African cultures and millions of innocent people from around the 1400s until today.

The African features of modern Brazil in general are confined to the basic physical appearance of much of the population, certain religious practices, and Brazilian music. I found that most of the African-descended people of Brazil live in impoverished conditions, while their light-complexioned and European-descended counterparts live in comparative luxury. While many of the Afro-Americans

Preface

retain some of their ancestral customs, they have relinquished a significant proportion of them in their attempts to overcome their economic condition.

The largest percentages of Afro-Americans in the Spanish-speaking countries of South America are found in Colombia and Venezuela. In these countries, too, the amount and quality of African retentions are directly correlated with the degree to which the African-descended people were excluded from the economy of the modern society. That is, those who are impoverished and uneducated frequently lived in their own enclaves in the undeveloped parts of the country and must rely on ancestral customs more compatible with their habitat and state of existence. However, the interior of Colombia houses a significant number of bush-dwelling Afro-Americans (so-called Maroons) who are descendants of rebellious slaves in that area.

During my search throughout South America, I concluded that the countries with the purest African-descended people in this hemisphere, both culturally and genetically, were Surinam* (formerly Dutch Guiana) and French Guiana. Surinam is located in the northeast corner of South America, between 2 and 6 degrees north latitude and 54 and 58 degrees west longitude. These two largely undeveloped countries, particularly Surinam, contain a significant number of people who by all appearances are as African today as were their ancestors three hundred years ago. They live in scattered villages from a few miles south of the Atlantic Ocean down to the Brazilian border. In Surinam, where their ancestors fought a successful one-hundred-year guerrilla war against their would-be European enslavers, these Afro-Americans of the bush have kept Africa alive in the New World more than any other group. They exist today as an independent nation-within-a-nation.

My research revealed that the African-descended people of the Surinam rain forest have been called many different names by different groups, depending on their interest and motivation. Djukas and Maroons are names used by anthropologists, missionaries, and the Dutch colonialists. They are called Bush Negroes or Djukas by the governments of Surinam and French Guiana. Many bush people reject these names as offensive and misleading. They refer to themselves collectively as the "river people," "bush people," or by their tribal names—Aucaner, Saramacca, Paramacca, Matawai, and Boni (there are five major tribal nations and one smaller one). We decided to refer to these people collectively as the Bush Afro-Americans. They are bush dwellers, and they are people of African origin

*The Republic of Surinam has officially changed the spelling of its name. It is now Suriname. This book was written before the change was made.

Preface

and American experiences. They share a common history with every other African-descended person in this hemisphere. In fact, they more than any of us today can lay claim to the title Afro-American. And since they represent a homogeneous group in terms of their general African origins and present habitat, we did not subdivide them into their separate nations or so-called tribes but rather described them as a single group as they are perceived by their countrymen.

I decided to conduct my studies among the Afro-Americans living in the interior of Surinam and then set about making plans to return to South America and live among them, to experience their culture and to learn what they were willing to teach me about themselves. I wanted my work to be systematic and scientific but also personal and brotherly. Moreover, I did not want to focus on those so-called Bush Negroes who live in the periphery of the bush, not far from Western civilization, who have been the focus of European and American anthropologists and have already welcomed Western gadgetry. I wanted to venture into the deepest part of the jungle to live among the bush people who wanted nothing to do with the outside world and have been essentially isolated. I wanted to find out how much of their original African culture they had retained because that is important to all Afro-Americans.

I longed to meet the most remote of these people. Would they be different in their thinking, their sense of unity and self-respect, from American blacks and, if so, how? What would be their concept of themselves, of the world around them? (In Brazil, I had met surprisingly many literate and nonliterate Afro-Americans who had no knowledge of the black presence in the United States.) I was determined to answer these and other questions firsthand and to share this information with other Afro-Americans when I returned.

In order to accomplish my mission I would have to obtain the necessary funds for transportation, supplies, and, once in Surinam, guides, bearers, and other assistants who could travel with the expedition. I began seeking financial support for my project from organizations, foundations, and groups, but without success. Funds for such a project might be obtained from several different agencies by anthropologists, but such funds were not available to me. I then decided that I would seek grant support for my expedition by proposing a study of the origins and scientific applications of medicinal plants used by the Bush Afro-Americans in healing and religion. But many of the people I approached suggested that my proposed project was basically anthropological and, as such, should be left to established anthropologists.

I was discouraged at every encounter but not deterred, and I finally decided to go ahead with my plans by using my savings and funds borrowed from my family. I invested in a 35 mm camera and a motion picture camera so that I could document various aspects of my interaction with bush people as well as scientific and cultural findings. I learned a very important lesson from this experience: When you want to do something and you know that your aims are sincere and moral, do not be discouraged by those who are threatened by your mission.

Some months before my departure, I decided that it would be good to have someone join me on the expedition who had scientific and cultural interests like mine. I approached several friends and colleagues with my idea, particularly those with scientific backgrounds, and extended invitations. Most of them thought I was unrealistic to be considering a trip into the South American rain forest, especially since I had little previous experience in jungle living. Some felt that this was "taking blackness a bit too far." Finally David L. Evans, an old friend who was then senior admissions officer at Harvard and an electrical engineer, agreed to join me. I told him that this would be an expedition to the most remote jungle villages of Surinam and French Guiana in South America to learn more about our people who had not lived under the physical and economic conditions we had here in the United States. From the first David was profoundly interested. I began to visit him daily to talk and exchange literature.

For many years I'd known David as a veritable storehouse of knowledge on U.S. black history and culture, and his developing interest in my project was related to his general interest in Afro-American culture. We found ourselves discussing the lives and stories of our grandparents and thought it interesting that neither my great-grandmother, who lived to be close to 100, nor his grandmother, who had died a few years later at 103, had to our knowledge retained any African language or culture. Yet during their lifetimes they had known ex-slaves who had been brought directly from Africa. David began reading material about the early Afro-Americans and their struggles against slavery. One night he announced that he would join me on the expedition but could only stay for two months. I was delighted to have found a person with such a profound sensitivity for the plight of Afro-American people, one who understood our desperate need for positive identities.

In June 1972 David and I set out on the most important journey of our lives. The trip was to take us to the most remote and unexplored regions of the South American rain forests, where we witnessed our history in living form. It was a very risky and dangerous undertaking, but it was worth every second. Our lives have been greatly enriched by this extraordinary experience, and we are very happy to be able to share it with other Americans. Since the begin-

Preface

ning we have made seven separate explorations into the South American rain forests to live with the Bush Afro-Americans.

The following pictorial essay condenses the experiences of those seven years into one long visit with the brothers and sisters who had been lost to us for so long. It is a candid and honest presentation of our experiences with the purest members of our family. It is the personal story of a 350-year reunion between two Afro-Americans from the United States and the people who represent the connecting link between U.S. blacks and Africans. It is not a typical academic's account of discovering an uncivilized and backward black tribe. We discovered an experience, we discovered friends and family, we discovered ourselves.

S. Allen Counter

Acknowledgments

We owe a great deal of gratitude to the African-descended people of the Suriname bush for their sincere generosity and tolerance and the wealth of wonderful experiences we were privileged to share with them. The paramount chieftains (*gramans*), Gazon, Aboikoni, and Aboni deserve special thanks for their hospitality to us. We are also indebted to members of the Suriname government who have over the years given us their support and encouragement: President Johan H. E. Ferrier, Ministers of Economics Just Rens and Eddy Bruma, Minister of Interior Olton van Genderen, and Prime Minister Henke Arron. Other helpful Suriname citizens were Joseph Tam, Baltus Loecum, Robin Dobru Ravales, Edward Danny Dens, Cyriel Karg, T. Van Ommeren, and W. Zalmijn.

We are sincerely grateful to the late Roy E. Larsen for his genuine interest in and support of our work. We are also most appreciative of the support of Dr. and Mrs. Edwin Land and the Rowland Foundation. We are indebted to Chase and Grete Peterson for their friendship, encouragement, and special interest in our work.

We would like to thank President Derek C. Bok of Harvard University for his special support. L. Fred Jewett and John E. Dowling of Harvard were also very helpful and supportive during the conduct of our work.

We are especially grateful to Tony Brown, executive producer of *Black Journal* and *Tony Brown's Journal* for his initial and long-term interest in our work. Mr. Brown introduced our work to the American public in a magnificently produced PBS national broadcast called "The Original Brother."

We owe a special debt of gratitude to Marvin Hightower of the Harvard News Office for an excellent introductory article on our work called "Africa in the New World" and his important contribution to one of our expeditions.

Special thanks to Anthony Bruce Jacobs who gave us invaluable technical assistance on several expeditions.

We would also like to thank the following persons for their special efforts and contributions to our Suriname projects over the years: Louis C. Brown, Leo H. Buchanan, Regina O. Counter, Ann J. Daniels, Letha Canada Evans, Mercedes S. Evans, Ernest J. Moore, Robert Nixon of ABC Sports, Mrs. Eddie Lee Pettis, Colin Turnbull, and the late Cornelius A. Askew, Jr.

I Sought My Brother

A History

Some Afric chief will rise, who scorning chains,
Racks, tortures, flames, excruciating pains,
Will lead his injur'd friends to bloody fight,
And in the flooded Carnage take delight;
Then dear repay us in some vengeful war,
And give us blood for blood, and scar for scar.
John Gabriel Stedman, 1796

Of all the literature we found during our initial research on the so-called Bush Negroes of Surinam, none was more impressive or affected us more profoundly than a book by John Gabriel Stedman, *Narrative of an Expedition against the Revolted Negroes of Surinam.* This two-volume treatise is an account by an eighteenth-century soldier who became an on-the-spot reporter of the events in Surinam from 1772 to 1777. Stedman described in vivid detail, including exquisite etchings, the arrival of Africans in Surinam, their treatment by European enslavers, and the escape of the Africans into the Surinam (and French Guiana) bush. He also gives a dramatic account of the guerrilla war waged by the Africans for their freedom from Euro-American domination. Although there were other excellent accounts of the same period in Surinam by the Dutchman Hartsinck and the Frenchman Fermin, we found Stedman's volumes more instructive. He provided essentially up-to-date maps of where the African freedom fighters had marched and detailed drawings of what the people should look like in these areas. All we had to do was to follow his maps into the most isolated sections of the country and seek out our brethren.

According to Stedman and other contemporary writers, rebel slaves of the seventeenth century rose up against the plantation owners, cast off their bondage, fled to the cover of the rain forest, and organized themselves into fighting units. They waged a guerrilla war against the Dutch colony of Surinam for over one hundred years. The magnitude and ferocity of their attacks were such that on several occasions the entire colony was feared lost to them.

While the exact date of the arrival of African slaves in Surinam is unknown, it is generally accepted that they were brought to that colony in the early 1600s. In 1650 an Englishman, Francis Willoughby, earl of Parham, established the first permanent European settlement. Twelve years later Charles II, king of England, granted a charter for Surinam to Willoughby and a Laurance Hyde.

The records of the first escapes from slavery in Surinam are vaguer than what is known about the arrival date of the first Africans. Nonetheless early flight to the thick jungle is borne out in "Essai Historique sur la Colonie de Surinam," by David Nassy et al., Paramaribo, 1788: "From the time of the English, even before the period of 1655, there had already been negro runaways in the woods."

Three years after Willoughby and Hyde assumed ownership of the colony of Surinam, England and Holland went to war for the second time, this time for two years (1665–1667). Two of its consequences were that the Dutch received Surinam in South America and the English received New Amsterdam (New York) in North America. Surinam was not expressly exchanged for New York as is popularly believed. The Treaty of Breda, which was signed by the Dutch and English on July 31, 1667, declared that all territories captured before May 10, 1667, would remain under the jurisdiction of the captors. Those territories captured after May 10 were to be returned to the sovereignty of the former owners. Dutch Vice-Admiral Abraham Cryssen had captured Surinam from the English on February 27, 1667, and, likewise, New Amsterdam was in the hands of the English prior to May 10, 1667.

Slaves had been escaping since the first arrivals in the colony; usually these were individual or small group efforts. But later attacks upon Surinam by the French altered the escape patterns, giving the slaves a chance for massive escape. The escaped slaves were mostly men, the memory of the overseer's lash fresh in their minds. Without many of the tools necessary for survival in the hostile jungle, they began by organizing themselves into raiding parties and carrying out hit-and-run attacks upon the plantations, primarily for supplies, but later to free African women.

The history of the bush women, like that of the men, is one of laudable courage and resilience. They endured great suffering and yet were at the forefront of the struggle to overcome the oppression of the Euro-American enslavers through revolution. Stedman's volumes are filled with examples of the inhuman treatment of African slave women by the enslavers. In fact, Stedman states that the first sight he beheld upon landing in Surinam was "a young female slave, whose only covering was a rag tied around her loins, which, like her skin, was lacerated in several places by the stroke of the whip. The crime which had been committed by this miserable victim of tyranny was the non-performance of a task to which she was apparently unequal, for which she was sentenced to receive two hundred lashes, and to drag, during some months a chain several yards in length, one end of which was locked around her ankle, and to the other was affixed a weight of at least a hundred pounds."

A History

Afro-American slave women and Indian slave women were subject to physical and sexual abuse at the slightest whim of the white enslavers. Stedman observed that "what is peculiarly provoking to them [the Afro-American family] is that if a Negro and his wife have ever so great an attachment for each other, the woman, if handsome, must yield to the loathsome embrace of an adulterous and licentious manager (overseer) or see her husband cut to pieces for endeavoring to prevent it."

This well-documented savage treatment of black women was perpetrated not only by white men. Many Euro-American women were reported to have indulged in the most atrocious and brutal acts against the enslaved women. In one instance, Stedman cites an act committed against a black slave woman and child in a boat by a white woman:

A Mrs. Sklr, going to her estate in a tent barge, a negro woman, with her sucking infant, happened to be passengers, and were seated on the bow, or fore-part, of the boat. The child crying from pain perhaps or some other reason, could not be hushed. Mrs. Sklr, offended by the cries of this innocent little creature, ordered the mother to bring it aft, and deliver it into her hands; then in the presence of the distracted parent, she immediately thrust it out at one of the tilt-windows, where she held it under water until it was drowned, and then let it go. The fond mother, in a state of desperation, instantly leapt over into the stream where floated her beloved offspring, in conjunction with which she was determined to finish her miserable existence. In this, however, she was prevented by the exertions of the negroes who rowed the boat, and was punished by her mistress with three or four hundred lashes for her daring temerity.

The atrocities led many slave women to commit suicide. But, many others fled the plantations and joined their revolutionary brethren in the bush, where they helped the men strike fiercely at their former enslavers.

In the battles against the Euro-American enslavers, the Bush Afro-American women fought alongside their men. In many cases when plantations were attacked and raided by the freedom fighters, the women assisted by acting as intelligence gatherers or by aiding their enslaved sisters to escape to the bush. In instances of military confrontation with army troops and mercenaries, many women were part of the front-line forces of the freedom fighters. There they fought valiantly, charging trained European soldiers and repelling them, fighting to the death, even when parts of their bodies had been blown off.

When freedom fighters raided the plantations, they took African women who were willing to flee to the bush, as well as those who were too frightened to escape. The white colonists viewed the freeing or capture of female slaves by the rebels an act of guerrilla warfare against the state because they considered slave women their property.

In the seventeenth and eighteenth centuries, the African slaves were classified according to color. Although most were pure African, many were the lighter complexioned result of forced miscegenation by Euro-American men. The offspring of these unions were referred to as mulattoes, samboes, quadroons and maesti. Stedman once said of Surinam that "Here, one meets not only with the white, the black, and the olive, but with the Samboe dark, and the mulatto brown, the maesti fair, the well-limbed quadroon." A mulatto resulted from the union of a white man and a black woman. A samboe was defined as "between a mulatto and a black, being of a deep copper-coloured complexion, with dark hair that curls in large ringlets." A quadroon resulted from the mating of a "white male and a mulatto female." A maesti (octoroon) was defined as "the offspring of a European [male] and a quadroon [female]." It is to be emphasized here that each of these mixtures resulted from the mating of a European, white male and a "colored" slave female. For as Stedman put it, "should it be known that a European female had intercourse with a slave of any denomination, she is forever detested, and the slave loses his life without mercy."

When regular militia and Dutch soldiers sent from Holland were ineffective in checking the constant raids that were devastating the colony, mercenaries were recruited from other European countries to aid in the suppression of the rebellion. Even the augmented forces of the colonial government could not stop the repeated attacks.

These black men and women were driven by the normal human longing for freedom, but in Surinam they had extra motivation: a desire to avenge some of the cruelest treatment of slaves in human history. Slaves had been mutilated at whim, killed or tortured for the slightest indiscretion, and often worked in 90°F sun until they dropped.

While rebel slaves waged successful attacks against them, the militia suffered from malaria, yellow fever, dysentery, jungle rot, and very poor discipline and morale. Military victory over the rebels seemed more remote with each passing day. Moreover, advanced military technology could not be used against the menacing rebels. Cannons, cavalry, and ships were ineffective in the thick jungles and rock-strewn rivers of Surinam.

The wiser members of the colonial government recognized that these black men and women would not cease their attacks until there was no threat to their freedom left in the colony. In 1684 the new Dutch governor, Cornelius van Aarssens, lord of Sommelsdyk,

A History

A physically abused
female slave.
(Stedman, 1796)

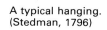

A typical hanging.
(Stedman, 1796)

6

A Bush Afro-American
freedom fighter.
(Stedman, 1796)

An eighteenth-century
mulatto woman.
(Stedman, 1796)

A ranger. One of the
hired slaves who
tracked African fighters
in exchange for their
own freedom.
(Stedman, 1796)

Surinam rain forest.

sought out the rebels at the Copename River to arrange a peace treaty. Luckily for the Dutch, the rebel slaves did not want to conquer the colony as had the French or the English; they only wanted to be left alone to live free in their bush habitat as they had in Africa. But if Lord Sommelsdyk's motives in making peace with the Copename Rebels were to discourage other uprisings, escapes and attacks, he was wrong. Many, many more were to come.

Over the next ten decades, attacks by the rebels grew in magnitude and frequency to such ferocity that the colony on several occasions was deemed lost to the rebels. Stedman reported, "The revolted negro slaves . . . for some time diffused a general terror over this settlement, and threatened its total loss to the states of Holland."

The slave trade was based on a belief by the enslavers that the Africans were inferior to the Europeans, but occasionally this arrogant prejudice verged on insanity. In October 1712, a French squadron chief, Jacques Cassard, invaded Surinam with approximately three thousand men and held the colony until December of that year. During the siege of Cassard, several of the Dutch slaveholders sent their women and children into the jungle under the protection of their slaves. The slaves were expected to return faithfully to bondage when the French were either repulsed or the hostilities were otherwise ended. The women and children were allowed to return unharmed from the periphery of the jungle when the fighting was over, but the slaves joined the rebels of the deep bush.

Cassard's two-month siege caused massive confusion in the colony, and thousands of slaves fled into the nearly impenetrable jungle to rebel hideaways. In 1726 there were approximately five thousand rebels in the bush and fifty thousand slaves on the plantations and in the capital. With such numbers, the rebels were now a formidable enemy capable of striking almost at will upon the five hundred plantations, and vanishing into the bush.

Many times plantation owners were thankful to have escaped with their lives, although their property was sacked and burned, as was revealed in this letter from a fleeing planter, cited by Stedman:

Sir,
   This is to acquaint you that the rebels have burnt three estates by your side, Suyingheyd, Peru, and L'Esperance, the ruins of which are still smoking; and that they have cut the throats of all the white inhabitants that fell in their way. As on their retreat they must pass close by where you are posted, be on your guard.—I am in haste.
                                        Your's & C.
                                        (Signed) Stoeleman

As a desperate countermeasure against the ever-mounting attacks of the rebels, in 1730 the colonists publicly executed eleven captured "rebels"—three men, six women, and two girls. The methods

A History

of execution are almost unthinkable in their cruelty: one of the men was impaled on a metal hook through his rib cage and left hanging for three or four days until death relieved him of his misery; two men were burned alive at the stake; the six women were broken upon the rack; and the two girls decapitated. These were not isolated examples and were considered routine and natural treatment of blacks.

Surely these barbarous acts must have burned themselves into the minds of all those slaves who witnessed them. Intended to suppress defiance and thoughts of escape, the executions must have forced the most timid among them to acknowledge that they must submit or defy. Many chose to join their brethren in the bush, carrying with them fresh thoughts of the executions and a hunger for revenge.

For the rebels, the news of the executions also produced the opposite of the effect intended by the colonists. Far from dampening their spirit of rebellion, it provoked attacks of even greater ferocity.

Rage and revenge on the part of the rebels begot the same from the colonists and, in turn, even greater rage from the rebels. Thus the cycle spiraled, increasingly favoring the rebels, until 1749. In that year the governor, Jan J. Mauritius, saw the futility of his situation and considered the possibility of making peace with the Saramacca rebels (named for the Saramacca River along which they settled). Over some strong opposition in his government, Mauritius's peace proposition won formal consideration. He sent a detachment of soldiers to seek out Captain Adu, paramount chief of the Saramacca, and to propose a peace treaty.

After a few skirmishes, the detachment reached Chief Adu's village. There the government offered independence and freedom forever to the rebels in exchange for a colony that would be free of their menacing raids. Moreover, the rebels would be served a yearly tribute beginning one year after the proposed treaty. This tribute would include guns, powder, shots, axes, saws, and other tools necessary to survive in the harsh jungle environment. Ceremonial gifts were exchanged: a silver-headed cane bearing the Surinam crest for Captain Adu and a bow and arrow set (personally carved, strung, and tipped by Adu) for the governor.

In 1750, one year after the tentative peace agreement with the Saramaccas, a military unit was sent to deliver the promised gifts to Chief Adu. Unfortunately a third party, Chief Zam Zam, entered the picture. Zam Zam, disgruntled because he had been neglected and left out of the peace negotiations, was so enraged by this slight that he attacked the delivering party, killed the whole detachment, and took the gifts for himself.

A History

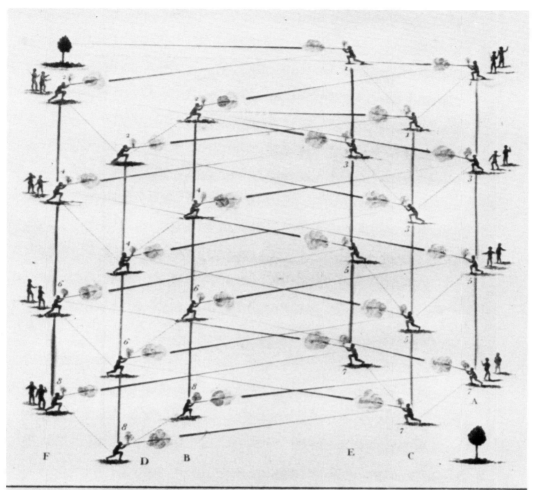

Manner of Bush-fighting by the African Negroes

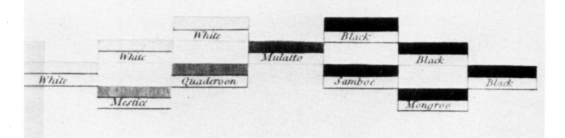

Gradation of Shades between Europe & Africa

Crossfire—a typical
battle tactic. (Stedman,
1796)

A sacred statue taken
from the Surinam rain
forest by a visitor in
the 1800s. (Courtesy of
the Harvard Peabody
Museum)

Meanwhile Chief Adu waited patiently for the promised gifts and, when none arrived, he concluded that he and his people were victims of still another one of the white man's tricks. He now reasoned that the one-year grace period had been a stalling tactic to give the colonists time to summon more troops from Europe and went to war again, this time more vengeful than before. This new Saramacca war raged until it was finally ended through a peace treaty in 1762. By that time Chief Adu was dead, and his people were led by Chief Willie.

The interim period between 1749 and 1762 was also the time of a major rebellion among the slaves of the settlements around the Tempati Creek. This uprising occurred in 1757, and these Tempati rebels fled and joined the many rebels who had settled near the Djuka Creek. Well armed and numbering, according to some estimates, nearly one thousand, this new group posed a threat to the colony worse than any it had previously known. After they had been successively defeated, the colonists found notes written by "Boston," a captain of the "negroes of Djuka," at some of the destroyed plantations, suggesting the rebels' willingness to begin peace talks.

The new governor, Wigbold Crommelin (Mauritius had been sent back to Holland in 1751 and three other men had briefly headed the government in the interim period), ordered his emissaries to reach these rebels and to suggest peace talks. The rebels agreed to talk but demanded that the Dutch serve them yearly with a list of essentials, including guns, shots, powder, and tools.

Following this agreement, Governor Crommelin dispatched two representatives, Abercrombie and Sober, to meet with Chief Araby, the paramount chief of the "negroes of Djuka," and to draw up the preliminaries of a treaty. This meeting was arranged for October 1759, the two men and their unit carrying along token gifts for the rebels, which included mirrors, combs, and scissors. Captain Boston was enraged and insulted by these unessential gifts; he had drawn up the list the year before and it included guns and ammunition. He wanted to hold Abercrombie, Sober, and their party as hostages until appropriate goods were delivered. At the strong urging of Boston's fellow Captain Quaco and the final authority of Chief Araby, the Abercrombie and Sober detachment was allowed to return to Paramaribo. With them they took a new list of demands for supplies from Chief Araby and his strong warnings that insults like the one that had just occurred could have ominous consequences.

As a condition of these preliminary peace talks, neither side was to take hostile action against the other for one year. During that year the supplies demanded by Chief Araby were to be sent. The

A History

year was uneventful except for a meeting in April 1760 to clarify points of the treaty. As promised, one year following the meeting between Abercrombie, Sober, and Chief Araby, a treaty was ratified between the colony of Surinam and the "negroes of Djuka."

It was a solemn occasion for the rebels, and they demanded that the treaty be ratified according to their tradition as well as the white man's. Each participant was required to slash his arm and shed a few drops of blood into a calabash gourd and onto the ground. The blood of the rebels and the colonists was mixed together with particles of earth and spring water. Everybody present, black and white, was required to drink from the gourd, and in so doing, swore an oath that would bring down the wrath of the Almighty on those who violated it. The 1762 peace treaty with the Saramaccas had been similarly concluded.

The same Chief Zam Zam who had disrupted earlier Saramacca peace talks made himself heard again. This time he attacked the detachment delivering materials to the Saramaccas and took the supplies but spared the troops. This time the survivors were able to inform Chief Willie and the Saramaccas that their failure to deliver the tribute was not deceit on the part of the colonial government.

One Captain Muzinga was not informed of Zam Zam's attack, and he thought this failure to deliver was a violation of the terms of peace already agreed upon. So Muzinga went to war attacking plantations, liberating slaves, and routing troops sent to capture him. In 1767 peace was declared with Captain Muzinga, whose descendants are known as the Matawais.

Many thought that the peace made with the Djukas, the Saramaccas and the Matawais would bring tranquility back to the colony. It did not. This small tropical slave colony had yet to experience the Cottica rebellions, named for the river along which several of the rebellions occurred. The new violence sent shock waves throughout the colony. This is how Stedman described it: "In 1772 they [the rebels] had nearly given the finishing blow to Surinam. At that period all was horror and consternation—nothing but a general massacre was expected by the majority of the inhabitants, who fled from their estates, and crowded to the town of Paramaribo for protection."

These violent eruptions were led principally by three rebels whose names would become synonymous with successful slave revolts in Surinam: Joli-Coeur, Baron, and Bonni. One of the tribes that lives today along the Surinam-French Guiana border is called the Bonni tribe, named for the famous rebel chieftain who led their ancestors in the freedom struggle. The terror heaped upon Surinam by these new rebels led the colonial government to take measures theretofore unthinkable: slaves would be recruited and armed to

A History

fight slaves. Many colonists shuddered at the thought, but the status of the colony was at stake.

In 1772 a group of two hundred slaves was enlisted for the purpose of fighting the rebels. They were designated as the "Corps of Free Negroes" and were selected from all of the plantations as the "best" slaves. Clearly the word "best" implied a strong loyalty to the slave owners, as well as mental and physical readiness to fight and recapture the rebels. These "Freed Negroes" also became known as "Rangers," and they were commanded by white "conductors." To distinguish them from the rebels, they were issued red caps, special breeches, and taught the shibboleth "Orange."

The Rangers enthusiastically fought the rebels to impress their conductors and took their zeal even further. To prove their bravery and loyalty to the colony, the Rangers were required to cut off the right hands of the rebels whom they killed. The hands were then barbecued or smoke-dried and delivered to the governor at Paramaribo, for which the rangers were rewarded twenty-five florins each.

Warriors reserve a special disdain for tribal members who side with the enemy. This is particularly true when two "tribes" are at war and the collaborators are members of a persecuted ethnic group. Often the hatred for the treasonous brethren is stronger than that for the enemy in general. In many instances, when the Surinam rebels attacked a government patrol and were in a position to fire indiscriminately upon the detachment, they chose instead to fire upon the rangers without hurting a single European.

Joli-Coeur, Baron, and Bonni may have made such effective rebel leaders because of the personal grudges they harbored for their former enslavers and for those who sided with the Europeans. As a child, Joli-Coeur had seen his mother ravished by the plantation manager and his father brutally flogged for attempting to rescue his mother. One day this same manager would die begging for his life at the hand of Joli-Coeur.

Baron had learned to read and write and had learned the skills of a mason while a slave. He had also been a "model" slave, traveling extensively with his owner. On one journey, his owner promised him his freedom upon their return to Surinam, but the owner went back on his word, refused Baron his freedom, and went even further in his treachery, selling Baron as mere chattel. Broken-hearted and dejected, Baron refused to work for his new owner and was consequently flogged in public. His bitterness intensified, and he fled to the bush "vowing revenge against all Europeans without exception." He swore that he would not die peacefully until he had "washed his hands in the blood of his former owner."

A History

Bonni had never been a slave. He had been born after his pregnant mother escaped from the plantation where she had been raped by her white enslaver. Bonni was therefore a mulatto and was "different" from the other black children with whom he grew up. A half-breed, he bore the mark of *bakrah* (the white man). It is not hard to imagine that this distinctive mark could have motivated him to excel and ultimately to become the leader of his people. This mark also drove him to hate Europeans with an all-consuming passion. He was known to punish his own men severly for uttering complimentary words about the Europeans. Moreover, Bonni did not trust new arrivals from the plantations. They had to serve a two-year probationary period during which they could not bear arms and were under constant surveillance. Joining Bonni's forces was so taxing upon the constitution and spirit of a new arrival that a few returned to their European owners. But when they returned to bondage they were tortured to death by the Europeans.

With these men and their followers in the woods threatening to strike the final blow to the colony, Surinam officials appealed to Holland for help again in 1772. In response, Holland sent five hundred mercenaries to the colony, under the direction of a Colonel Louis Fourgeoud. John Gabriel Stedman served as a captain in this mercenary force.

The mercenary unit arrived in Surinam on February 2, 1773, and one of Stedman's first sights revealed to him that the rebels were nothing like the mutinous riffraff to be found in many European military units of that era. These black men and women were reacting to a system of servitude that killed or maimed so many slaves that the colony required at least twenty-five hundred replacements from Africa each year. The fact that the overall slave population remained around fifty thousand for many years meant that Surinam went through a whole "complement of slaves in twenty years!"

The rebels, led by Bonni, Baron, and Joli-Coeur, were not a mob or a gang of unorganized rabble; they had become military strategists of the highest order. After Fourgeoud's troops had been fooled one night by a fake battle that camouflaged the escape of a whole village of seemingly trapped rebels, Stedman wrote, "This was certainly such a masterly trait of generalship in a savage people, whom we affected to despise, as would have done honour to any European commander, and has perhaps been seldom equalled by more civilized nations."

In 1779 a miniature "Wall of China" was built around most of the cultivated portion of Surinam. Known as the *Cordon Path,* it became a strain to the colony's resources; large numbers of soldiers were required to guard it, and its construction and maintenance were a heavy economic burden. This barrier reduced the frequency of the raids but did not stop them.

A History

Holland poured more men and arms into Surinam as its losses mounted. The climate and disease continued to match the rebels in claiming European casualties. This strain on the budget and personnel of the colonial government provoked a strong debate between Governor Jean Nepveu and Colonel Louis H. Fourgeoud as to how best to secure the colony against the rebels.

Bonni and his people finally withdrew into French Guiana, apparently tired of the long years of fighting. Governor Nepveu was satisfied, but Colonel Fourgeoud was not. He wanted to pursue Bonni into French Guiana even if that meant risk of provoking an international incident with the French government. The governor's side prevailed and confrontation was avoided.

Fourgeoud and his surviving troops (including Stedman) departed Surinam for Holland on April 1, 1778, leaving behind a tenuous peace and hundreds of dead comrades. Many of the survivors were permanently crippled or of broken health and had little hope of surviving very long. Among them was Colonel Fourgeoud himself, who died soon after his return to Europe.

Bonni and his people were not heard from again until the late 1780s when he crossed over from French Guiana and attacked some of the colonial estates.

In the early 1790s Bonni entered a dispute with the neighboring Djukas, and a fight ensued. Bonni was killed but a great deal of mythology surrounds his death. The Bonni tribe claims that the Djukas did not kill Bonni. The Djukas say otherwise. Legend has it that the Djukas cut off Bonni's head and were traveling down-river with it for a secret burial. But when they reached a certain spot on the river, the head leapt out of the boat and disappeared in the water. Extensive diving and searches failed to retrieve Bonni's head. The place where this mystical incident is supposed to have occurred is called *Bonni Doro,* and when passing it one is not supposed to utter the name of the famous rebel. To do so will summon bad spirits.

From the late 1790s until today, the bush dwellers have lived in peace in their own world, with little or no contact with outsiders. While some have migrated from the bush to the coastal towns over the last century, most have gone deeper into the rain forest, isolated from the rest of the world.

A History

The Reunion

Using Stedman as our major reference and guide, we set out to find the people whom he had described almost two centuries earlier. Would they still exist in the remote pockets he had indicated on his maps? Could we find them by traveling deep into this virtually unexplored part of Amazonas? Would they still be the same as they were two hundred or more years ago, or would they be more like many of their impoverished and poorly assimilated black brethren in the local towns and cities of Surinam? All of these questions were in our minds as we prepared to leave the United States for Surinam.

Paramaribo, the colonial Dutch capital of Surinam, was as hot and humid as our research had suggested it would be. But the surprise of our first visit was the fact that many of the city's buildings were at least two hundred years old and still in use. Some we even recognized from Stedman's book, and of these the one most interesting to us was Fort Zelandia, which had been converted to a museum.

This three-hundred-year-old structure was the major landing site for many of the slave ships during the peak of the slave trade. It also served as a holding pen for newly arrived slaves until they were sold at auctions. Even today some of its dark, dank cells are intact, and the neck, wrist, and ankle shackles worn by the slaves are displayed. Among these are heavy wrought-iron neck rings with spokelike rods that protrude approximately eighteen inches out from the wearer's neck. At the ends of the rods are hooks that would snag on bushes if a slave tried to escape by running into the thick jungle. Wearing the heavy neck ring gave a slave the wretched appearance of wearing a kind of wagon wheel having the spokes but lacking the outer ring.

Holding one of the neck rings in our hands and later examining some of the other manacles, we recognized a strange coincidence: one of our first sights in Surinam, like that of Stedman two centuries earlier, was a jolting introduction to the stark brutality of slavery in that country.

Fort Zelandia with its grim reminders of slavery and the other eighteenth-century buildings still in use had their positive effects upon us as well. They verified the accuracy of many of Stedman's drawings and descriptions. Because the buildings had changed so little, and the relics at the museum bore out Stedman's 1770s description, we wondered

Counter and Evans prepare to fly into the rain forest in small bush plane.

City of Paramaribo.

President's mansion.

Section of Fort
Zelandia where the
slaves were held upon
arrival in Surinam.

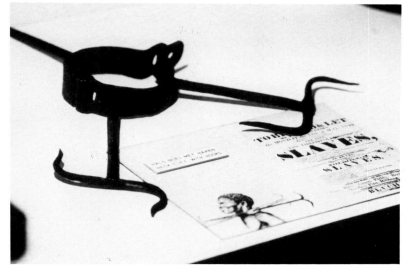

Typical neck cuff which
slaves were forced to
wear.

whether we would find the descendants of the rebel slaves in the rain forest equally unchanged.

Stedman's maps and the modern ones we purchased in Paramaribo seemed to indicate that most of the Bush Afro-Americans were located deep in the rain forest, hundreds of miles from the city, and that the more remote settlements in which we were interested could be reached only by river. Our initial plans were to find an experienced guide and a sturdy canoe so that we could paddle up one of the Surinam rivers until we had reached the hidden villages of the deep bush, and then hike by foot into the rain forest, down near the Brazilian border. We had come prepared with backpacks, hunting knives, a powerful hunting bow, a wealth of bush camping paraphernalia, and enough processed and canned food to last us about a month.

Our travel plans first had to be cleared by the interior ministry of the Surinam and French Guiana governments because certain borders of Surinam are contested by the neighboring countries and sometimes are sites of armed conflict. We met with a number of cabinet ministers, including the ministers of interior, economics, and development, telling them about our interest in searching out the Bush Afro-Americans of the rain forest and describing our plans. The ministers seemed at once confused and proud. On one hand they wondered why American scientists were interested in chancing the dangers of unfamiliar jungle just to visit the remote, tribal people of the interior. On the other, they said that they were proud to see that young, professional Afro-Americans were interested in this aspect of our mutual history. It was clear that they were pleased to have us pursue our research, and they expressed great pleasure in seeing "us" conducting cultural studies on Surinam's African-descended population.

The ministers agreed to deliver our plans to the president of Surinam, Dr. Johan H. E. Ferrier, for final approval. A day later, we were summoned to the presidential mansion. With President Ferrier and the cabinet ministers, we discussed our motivation and aims and their wish to protect the welfare of the bush dwellers by screening persons who enter the interior. We appreciated their concern about the well-being of the bush inhabitants and were impressed with the enlightened attitudes of these Afro-American men and women who

The Reunion

Counter and Evans discuss expedition plans with Surinam's President Johan H. E. Ferrier.

govern one of the most interesting and important countries in the Americas. (Surinam is a major supplier of bauxite, or aluminum, to the United States and Europe.)

President Ferrier finally gave us the government's blessings and later helped us to locate a guide and translator, a man who had been in the very deep bush and who had a reasonably good knowledge of the bush language. Finding a guide had proven to be difficult; few people from Surinam had ever ventured into the very deep rain forest. Most of the high government officials admitted that they had never traveled beyond the periphery of the jungle. The government extended its generosity even further by providing us with an airplane, pilot, and fuel to get us into the jungle and save us many days of travel by boat. The plane would take us to a missionary outpost in the jungle interior where there was a recently cut grass landing strip. At that point our guides would hire canoes and boatmen to transport us and our supplies to the jungle interior. We never asked for these gifts (which would have cost us thousands of dollars) but accepted them gladly.

The government's only request was that we show the utmost deference and respect for the bush people and their ways and that we obey their laws. They explained that the bush people who now lived at the edge of the cities (where

The Reunion

they had migrated from the bush over the past one hundred years) were reluctant to receive outsiders and could be dangerous if they felt violated. While they had little information on the Bush Afro-Americans of the deep jungle interior, they felt that these more isolated people could be very dangerous if their rules were violated. In any case they were beyond the reach of the laws of Surinam for all practical purposes. The president could give us permission to enter the bush, but he could not grant us permission to enter the villages of the bush. Only the bush people could do that, and only they could protect us during our sojourn in their territory.

Our journey into the jungle was delayed by heavy rains for several days, so we spent this time in Paramaribo studying our maps, compasses, and camera equipment. At the same time we learned that most city-dwelling blacks knew less about the Bush Afro-Americans than we did. Most of the population of Surinam (and French Guiana) live in the coastal cities, not far from the Atlantic. The Afro-American city dwellers are mostly descendants of plantation slaves who did not resist slavery but were freed by the emancipation proclamation of July 1, 1863, six months after the American proclamation. In appearance and complexion most of the people in the cities and towns are indistinguishable from Afro-Americans in the United States. They range in skin color from very dark (with Africanoid features) to very light complexioned (with European or African features). Those of lighter complexion have for centuries considered themselves somewhat superior to their darker-colored compatriots and were accorded certain advantages by the ruling Europeans. We recognized this pattern, but here in Surinam, the color hierarchy was still as primitive as it was in the United States in the 1920s. With few exceptions the darker-colored people were the poorest, lived in the most economically depressed areas, and had the most menial jobs. The lighter-colored Afro-Americans and the Asians were almost invariably better off economically and socially, and the whites had complete control of the economy. Yet most of the Surinam Afro-Americans accepted this pattern of life as natural.

Many of the older Surinamers (even those of darker skin color) refer to themselves as "creoles" and speak positively of their mixed white heritage. Most of them had never ventured into the jungle and therefore had not seen a Bush

The Reunion

Afro-American village. Some referred to the bush people by such terms as "savage," "backward," and "uncivilized runaways," or worse. Many wondered why we would be interested in these "primitive" people. They constantly warned us of the hazards of the jungle and the unpredictable "savagery" of the bush natives. We also met a large group of Afro-Americans in the city who had never entered the jungle but who had a great deal of love and respect for the bush dwellers. They knew the legends of the bush freedom fighters and were proud of their rebel history. For example, during our meeting with the government officials we learned that the Surinam Army had recently named its main military headquarters after an eighteenth-century rebel village called Boo Coo (which means, "I shall moulder before I shall be taken"). Fort Boo Coo, as it is now called, is a symbol of pride to the Surinam people.

When the hard rains ceased, we prepared to enter the deep jungle interior but learned that the rains had left the recently cleared grass runway unfit for landing our small plane. The soil under the landing strip was extremely soft, which made our chances for a safe landing very slim. So we decided to fly to another small, missionary-built landing strip about one hundred miles into the jungle and travel the rest of the way by hired canoe.

When the small plane had gained about three thousand feet, we could readily see the outlines of the coastal towns and the capital city. The muddy Atlantic was to the north, the dense rain forest to the south. Surinam, like neighboring French Guiana, has kept its lush green interior intact and even today is what industrial expansionists call undeveloped. Aside from clearings for the large bauxite mining operations, the dense, uninterrupted jungle forest appears some twenty miles inland. At about fifty miles inland the jungle is so thick as to be virtually impenetrable. Even today the rivers are the only pathways through the forest, just as they were three centuries ago when they served as highways to freedom for the escaped slaves. As we looked down, we could see a large river cutting its way through a stubborn green jungle like a giant sine wave.

After an hour of flying we were more than one hundred miles into the jungle and were able to spot small villages, each consisting of ten to twenty grass huts and a few tin-

The Reunion

roof houses. The villages tend to be built at the head of rapids, a habit developed during the freedom wars so that the pursuing European soldiers and mercenaries could be sighted and attacked during portage. The huts, our first real taste of the cultural preservation here, were the classical West-African-styled grass huts that have been built for centuries. We were delighted not to have discovered the shantytown, wooden shacks that we had expected.

As our plane landed on the small bumpy landing strip in the middle of a jungle clearing, several small children wearing loincloths came out to meet us. We were told that they were the children of the people who lived in the neighboring villages, a people already touched by modern Western society. Our goal lay further inland, with the most isolated of the bush people. We unloaded the plane while our guide set out to locate and hire a boat and boatmen familiar with the rivers in the deep bush interior. He returned with six short, muscular black men who appeared to be in their late thirties and one older man. They looked to us West African. Introducing us, our guide said that these men would provide us with two large dugout canoes, in which they would take us into the deep jungle interior. They left, returning promptly in colorful, thirty-foot-long canoes to a point in the river near our supplies. The canoes, which had been hand-paddled traditionally, were modified in the rear so that the men could attach outboard motors obtained from the new missionary outpost. These large motors were to save us days of travel time. We packed our supplies, equipment, barrels of engine fuel, and other provisions into the dugouts.

Neither of us could have predicted just how the next few hundred miles and few days would affect and indeed change our lives. In the first few hours we were on the river moving south toward Brazil; upstream, we felt as though we were being swallowed by this awe-inspiring rain forest and knew we could never escape without assistance. The feeling grew as time wore on, and we traveled for several days, stopping only to refuel our outboard motors and eat. Our supply of canned and dried foods was small and, wanting to conserve it, we supplemented our diet with coconuts and fresh fruits. The boatmen had brought along their own native food and refused to experiment with ours.

The Reunion

Two large dugouts
used for transport into
deep rain forest.

Rough rapids in
Surinam river.

Rife with dangerous rapids and large rocks, the rivers were negotiable only to the skilled men who had memorized its hazards. We got very little rest because of our fear of capsizing; the rivers are filled with unusually large piranha, which Surinamers call sweet-water sharks.

The natives said that if the boat capsized and we drowned, it might be because the river god wanted us. Still, they said they would forever feel guilty if they brought us to a watery end, so we traveled only by day, sleeping in riverside clearings at night. In the dugouts we kept ourselves ready for any eventuality by removing our boots and hanging our canteens and compasses around our necks.

As we traveled deeper into the jungle interior, the river became more violent in its rapids and swells. Some of the rapids almost threw us out of the boat. Suddenly the boatmen started to yell, *"Topoo, topoo, topoo,"* meaning, halt, look out! Our boat was going into a spin in the most active part of the rapids. It was actually being thrown back and against large rocks by the powerful current. We had to hold on to the sides of the boat to avoid being pitched out. At the front of the boat, one of the boatmen was frantically smashing his long pole (called a *kulu* stick) into the water trying to push us away from the rocks. But his pole kept slipping—it was no use. The rear engine fell silent—the propeller had hit a rock and broken a pin.

For the first time since we had begun the trip, some of our boatmen seemed to be unnerved by what was happening. But they never really lost their composure; rather they seemed surprised. The boat hit a large boulder in the center of the rapids and was spun a full 180 degrees. Water slammed into the boat with such force that many of our supplies were shaken loose. With no motor power, the boatmen had to paddle furiously because we were now being forced back downstream by the current at an unbelievable speed. The boatmen threw us our paddles, and we too tried to steer the large dugout around the sharp, pointed rocks, alternating between stalling positions and fast paddling in an effort to guide the boat safely while we were sped along at an uncontrollable rate.

All of a sudden, the older man who had been sitting under the canopy on the boat—a rather quiet, dignified man of small stature who was native to the bush country—leapt up,

The Reunion

grabbed a kulu stick from the floor of the boat, and began hitting the water with powerful, rapid motions. He took control of the boat and its crew, shouting directions and orders: now left, now right, now forward. The other boatmen had utmost confidence in him, following his directions precisely. The old man's tattered T-shirt became soaking wet, his powerful muscles bursting through the cloth. He was a masterful figure as he directed the boat crew by words and us by hand gestures.

Finally our boat began to slow down, and we were safely through the worst of the rapids. But we had traveled backward about two miles. As we passed the last whirlpool, the old man pointed his hand toward a small opening in the bush at the edge of the river. We paddled the boat to this little clearing and all gave huge sighs of relief. We felt empty, exhausted both emotionally and physically. Yet there had been a certain exhilaration in it all. We felt as if we had been put to some test, somehow initiated. We were proud of ourselves for sticking it out—we wanted to push on, to challenge the rapids again.

The boatmen got out of the boat to repair the engine propeller, standing unafraid, waist deep in the piranha-infested water. The boat itself was in good shape. It was a well-designed dugout tree and virtually indestructible. The powerful old man who had brought us safely through the rapids quietly returned to his seat under the canopy. Speaking through our interpreter, he said that the waters were unusually high this time of the year because of heavy rains and that the engine propeller had simply lost a pin when it struck a sharp rock; it would be repaired in about an hour. He said that once the engine was repaired we would approach the rapids from a slightly different direction, this time through heavy overlying bush but quieter water. Our only concern now was for the large snakes we had heard about back in Paramaribo, snakes that often fall into the boats as they pass under heavy vines and thick foliage. The Surinam jungle is teeming with them, including the giant anaconda and the deadly bush master.

The engine repaired, we headed upstream. We moved along another path, several meters to the right of the original. This path also had quick rapids, but the large rocks were fewer and the current not as strong. We helped with the pad-

The Reunion

Boatman uses *kulu*
stick to guide boat
through dangerous
rapids.

31

Boa constrictor on
river bank.

Young bush girl
startled by the sight of
the arrival party.

dling. The *kulu* man at the front of the boat cleared the thick brush overhead as we moved along the narrow river path. We kept watching for snakes in the limbs that barely missed our heads. Small monkeys were scurrying about, and large birds took to the air as the noise of our outboard engine and paddles came closer.

We spent the next two days traveling upstream in the rough river, not encountering a soul. Although exhausted, we stopped only to eat and rest, pushing forward toward the village of Topēkē, which the older man had told us about.

Two hundred miles into the deep rain forest, not far from neighboring Brazil, we rounded a sharp bend that jutted out into the river, like a small island with trees, and spotted something moving several yards ahead of us. We thought that it might be an animal because we had seen a few large and small animals moving about during our long trip. Our only worry with land animals was the possibility of meeting South American leopards or jaguars, which still thrive in this area and, at over five hundred pounds, represent a formidable threat. We raised our cameras hoping for the sight of a jaguar or other large animal, and what we saw as we cleared the overhanging foliage literally mesmerized us.

Standing several yards ahead of us was a young girl who looked so thoroughly African that she might have been standing on the banks of the Niger or the Congo or some other African river. Her color was deep black, her hair braided in rows, and she was naked to her waist with a loin-cloth around her lower abdomen. She wore colorful bracelets and anklets, much like those worn by the natives throughout West Africa.

We could not contain our delight at this evidence that we had found the culture we sought. We expressed our excitement so loudly that the child immediately spotted us and ran into the bush, but not before we could snap a photograph of her. We had never expected the people to be this classical, this different in their dress, this purely African and isolated from the outside world. Overjoyed, we knew we had to be cautious; we did not want to breach any rules or frighten anyone else by our enthusiasm. And we did not want to provoke any unreceptive behavior on the part of the people.

Just ahead of the spot where we had first seen the girl, we could see a portion of a thatched roof village. From the river

The Reunion

it seemed to hide behind a small clump of trees. The scene was right out of Stedman's book. Our boatmen cut the engine and began to paddle slowly along the river. We saw several people paddling about in small, colorful canoes; they studied us intensely as we passed. Some boats contained a man, a woman, and children, others only women or a man, sometimes with a bow and a hunting dog sitting at the point of the prow of the boat. At that moment it seemed that for every mile we had traveled into the rain forest we had traveled back about a year in time, until we had gone back more than two centuries. Farther upriver near the head village we saw further evidence that little had changed since Stedman's time. Stedman had drawn a picture of a typical Bush Afro-American woman in 1772 that summarized the contemporary dress, the method of balancing large bundles on heads, and the method of carrying infants. This picture had stayed in our minds. Two hundred years later, standing on the river bank just above us as our boat slowly neared land, we saw this same woman. In a way, it was as if she had stepped right out of his pages. If this stunning bush woman were to don Western clothes and appear in any American city, she could not be distinguished from other Afro-American women. Yet she had never heard of America, or Afro-America, for that matter. We later learned that when asked about herself she would give her name, her nation (tribe), and tell that she is an African whose ancestors had defeated *bakrah* (whites) and led their people to this land to be free. The peoples' poise, their confidence, their beauty, their African-ness was something to behold.

The young woman stopped to stare at us in defiance. She was not posing for a photograph but wondering about those little devices we were aiming at her. She immediately spoke in a soft but firm voice, pointed to the cameras and shook her head, "*Una pura, una pura,*" While we did not understand her language, we understood the message—"Don't aim those objects at me!" Immediately our interpreter told us to stop taking photographs until we had been given permission by the people of the village.

Three *bahjahs* or lieutenants came from their thatched palm huts in the village clearings down to the river where we were waiting in our boats. They approached us rather suspiciously but civilly. Our interpreter spoke up, "*Wike ba*"

The Reunion

(Greetings brothers). He went on, "We have come to visit your land. These men who are leading us are Africans also. They are Africans from a place called America, the United States." They stared at us even more cautiously. The small children crowded around our boat. One of the bush men smiled and said something to our interpreter that caused everyone to burst out in laughter. We did not understand but laughed in relief. The man came forward, shook our hands, and asked us to step out of the boats onto their shore. When we asked our interpreter what had been funny, he replied, "The *bahjah* wondered why, if you were African, you wear the clothes and other accoutrements of *bakrah*." We laughed again, but with a little embarrassment this time.

We were told to wait at the river until one of the village leaders came to escort us into the village. By this time men, women, and children had gathered at the river banks, many paddling by boat from neighboring villages when they heard that strangers had come. We got out of our boat and greeted them. They were friendly but very reserved.

Finally a village headman came to the river and asked us to follow him to the head village. As we walked up a small path to the village, which was hidden behind dense foliage, we passed under several palm fronds that hung across the path on tall poles. We were politely told to walk under these palm fronds and not around them. The villagers watched us to be certain that we obeyed their instructions. Later we asked about the significance of these palm fronds and were told that these structures, called *azang pau,* are sacred, and everyone entering the village must pass under them in order to have all evil spirits removed from their bodies and souls.

Our entire party was led down a long path toward the center village by the *bahjah,* with several curious youngsters following closely behind. We came upon a large clearing, were directed into its center, and had our second shock of the day. We stared incredulously as we slowly walked into this large "primitive" village. It was something out of another time, another place. Never had we dreamed of seeing such thatched-roof houses, fantastic wood-carved decorations, beautiful people wearing loin cloths: it was as if we had stepped into the fictional time machine and pressed the button for Africa of the sixteenth or seventeenth centuries. The village was called Pokaytee, which means "I shall retreat no further," so

The Reunion

Statue at river's edge protects village against evil intruders.

Mother and son transporting food in boat.

named hundreds of years ago during the freedom struggles. All of the villages had been given names that at once suggested poetry and defiance. Of the village names Stedman had written,

These appellations were all very expressive indeed; and as they may serve in some measure to elucidate our enquiries concerning the negro nations, I have thought proper to give them a place in this narrative, with their meaning in an English translation; viz . . . Gado Saby—God only knows me and none else. Cofaay—Come try me, if you be men. Tessee See—take a tasting, if you like it. Mele me—Do disturb me if you dare. Boosy Cray—The woods lament for me. Kebree—Hide me, o thou surrounding verdure.

We felt we had found pure Africa, right out of John Gabriel Stedman's drawings. The people and the village were as African as anything that can be found in most of the African continent today. The people began to crowd around us, people who were healthy, statuesque, and vibrant. It was obvious that they had adapted well to their new world and were in charge of their own destinies. We were thinking, "My God, my God, we have found our living ancestors, our preslavery blood line, still alive and well and proud. How could so much of our history have been here so long and we not know about it?" We were thoroughly pleased with what we had found, but our excitement was complicated by a kind of cognitive confusion: our eyes kept telling us that we were in Africa, but in our minds we knew that we were in South America.

We were shaken back into reality as the *bahjah* told us to take seats and wait until the head chieftain, the council of elders, and other villagers could be assembled. We would have to introduce ourselves to the village formally, state our reasons for visiting, and request permission to stay. We sat on small wooden stools called *bangis,* seats magnificently carved from a single piece of wood of a shape, structure, and decoration that are West African, specifically, Akan, Ghanaian.

The crowd grew but kept a safe distance from their new visitors. Only a few of the curious children ventured close enough to probe at our cameras and other paraphernalia. The wait was longer than we had expected—over an hour and a half—and we occasionally played with a curious child or just talked with our interpreter. This was our first experience with bush time or the fact that nothing and no one

The Reunion

rushes in the jungle. Everyone takes his time, and there is none of the frenetic rush-rush that we have grown accustomed to in our modern, technological society. Our hosts made us comfortable during our long wait by passing out fresh coconuts with cool, sweet juice and tasty pulp.

Finally we spotted the dignified, silver-haired elders heading toward us, followed by a small entourage. The crowd became silent, and we were asked to stand and greet the new arrivals. There was no question about who was in charge: the elders had the appearance of leaders and statesmen, pillars of the community. They were tall, proud, and confident. If they had been transplanted into the American South where we grew up, they would have been heads of the church, the deacons, the people who selected the minister, the kind who gave young people advice and formed the political leadership of the community.

The group came forward to greet us, but from some distance and with hands at their side. Our interpreter introduced us and himself to the leaders and explained the nature of our visit. We could not understand the language, but they seemed to be cordial hosts. The language intrigued us. We could hear what we thought to be several African languages plus several European-sounding words, notably Dutch and English.

We were asked by the elders to sit while the village council or *bossiah* prayed for the village and the visitors. We took our seats as the elders and an *obeah* man (holy, medicine man) entered a tall rectangular shrine about six feet high, ten feet wide, and ten feet deep. The shrine was covered with holy banners and the skulls of dead animals, and in the center there was a large wooden statue of a man's head. They all knelt as the chieftain led them in prayer. His prayer was punctuated by refrains like *"Eeua, eeba, daso,"* translated "Oh yes, yes, brother, that is true." There were humming and moaning sounds reminiscent of those heard during religious services in southern black churches. Throughout the prayers libations from a bottle of spirits were slowly poured onto the ground during every statement. [In this way you give unto God that which is important to you and that which is so powerful that it can take over your head, but not God's.]

The Reunion

We learned from our interpreter that the leaders were praying for the well-being of the village and thanking God for the new "African" visitors. However, they were also praying that the visitors came with goodwill in their hearts and did not bring disease or ill will to their land. Upon hearing this, we looked at each other with a real concern for our own well-being. Would we do anything that would suggest that we had brought ill will? Would our motives be misinterpreted? What would happen to us if they perceived us as evil or as couriers of ill will? Would they harm us? What had happened to other outsiders who were thought to be evil influences?

Prior to visiting the deep interior we had heard that a white adventurer somewhere in the peripheral jungle area near a mining town had to be rescued from a missionary outpost by police guards from the city. He was thought to have been implicated in the death of some older person who died mysteriously after his arrival. Also we had heard of the hatred that some of the natives in the peripheral bush (not far from the towns) harbor for white researchers whom they said had "spoiled some of their young women" or "asked them too many personal questions." We knew one thing for certain: if something went wrong there was no way out of this jungle without these peoples' help. It would take us from five to ten days to paddle back to a town at the edge of the rain forest. We were not in the peripheral bush but in the deep, remote jungle areas where few outsiders had ever set foot and where the people were isolated from the laws of the outside world. Yet while we had a mild concern that our motives would be misunderstood, we were not frightened of these proud people. We were awed by them. We trusted that they operated on a simple human rule: if we respected them they would respect us.

The council ended the prayers and came out of the shrine. They looked carefully at us as they directed the *bahjahs* to place our seats in a circle around the front of the religious shrine. The gathering villagers were so quiet that we had not seen them arrive. They appeared and stood near us. The headman, a silver-headed, African-looking man named Captain Kasea, said he would speak to our group in a *krutu.* A *krutu* is the most formal of the bush methods of group inter-

The Reunion

actions. It is used only in situations of gravity such as meeting with officials sent by the government of Surinam (although the president and ministers of Surinam had never ventured this far into the jungle), the selection of leaders, instances of judicial decisions, in meetings with outsiders, and other serious matters. The *krutu* can be traced back to the days of their ancestors' initial escape to the bush when they held meetings with the Surinam government's military representatives. During the *krutu,* one never speaks directly to the chieftain. One talks to and looks directly at an appointed go-between, or *bahjah.* To the go-between we said, "*Bahjah,* could you tell the chieftain that we have met with the president of Surinam in Paramaribo. He has given us permission to enter the bush and meet with the people of this river. However, he has said that the permission to enter the villages can only be granted by the bush people themselves. The president sends his regards and hopes that the chiefs and all of the bush people are blessed by good spirits." Throughout the conversation the *bahjah* affirmed each statement by uttering *eeya, eeya, eeya* at the end of each expression.

During this entire process, the chieftain and other elders studied the facial expressions, gestures, and words of the speaker carefully, while he talked to the third party, not looking directly at the chieftain. They said that this way they can scrutinize the speaker carefully to see if he is being truthful or if he is lying. We were most pleased with the inherent equality of this model when we learned that the chieftain offered us the same courtesy when he spoke to us through his *bahjah* and allowed us to examine the details and nuances of his expressions. His *bahjah* punctuated his statements with *eeya, eeba, daso,* my leader. We decided that we would first explain to the headman and entire village who we were and where we came from.

Counter said to the interpreter (who acted as our *bahjah*), "*Bahjah,* please tell the chieftain that we are an African-descended people too—we are African-Americans. Our ancestors were the same as those of the people of this great bush nation. Our ancestors were forcibly taken from their communities in Africa and brought to this part of the world to provide free labor for Europeans. They were taken to a northern land, far from here. [Counter then drew a map of South

America, Africa, and the United States on the ground in front of the chieftain.] Most of them died in the process, but many survived the subhuman conditions of the trip across the ocean and subsequent enslavement. We are the descendants of those Africans just as you are. We are your brothers, you are our brothers and sisters; we are all part of the same family, from the same ancestors; we have been looking for you and we have found you."

The entire village fell silent as our interpreter put this message across to the headman and elders assembled before us. As we looked around, we could observe that the villagers stared at us more and more incredulously as the message became clearer. Most of the women in the village stood together just outside of the *krutu* circle and in front of the seventeenth-century thatched roof huts. They gazed at us with sheer disbelief as our interpreter continued to translate the message.

Counter continued, "We have come to your land to the deep interior of the rain forest to learn what you have preserved from Africa. We would like permission to stay in your village for several weeks in order to learn more about your people, to study your ways, what you have kept alive from our ancestors in Africa."

The headman and council members exchanged glances. They seemed to find our story plausible.

Evans spoke: "*Bahjah,* could you tell the headman and the villagers that in our land the African-American people have trouble with their identity. They have lost almost all of the old African customs and language. We would like to take back information about you—how your ancestors fought the European enslavers and won their freedom before they lost their culture. We would like to take our findings about your culture to show our people in the United States. They would be proud to know about you."

The council members began to mumble among themselves as the interpreter delivered the last messages. They seemed pleased but confused by our statements.

Evans continued, "The way you have chosen to live here in your own nation—the elaborate and peaceful organization of your society—is important for our people to know about. In our country many of our people live in large, crowded areas and do great harm to each other. I'm told that

The Reunion

Counter asks
permission to stay
in village.

Evans explains
research interests.

The group of elders
assembled for the
introductory *krutu*.

you don't have that here; you don't harm each other, you support each other. So if we are given permission to stay, we hope to learn about those things and teach them to our people in the United States."

After a long hiatus and some discussion among themselves, the headman spoke softly to the silver-haired elders on his left and right, and they nodded as if they had agreed upon a decision. Through the *bahjah,* the headman spoke in a serious, inquisitive manner to us and our interpreter. The interpreter was laughing softly at the headman's statement. We were perplexed by his laughter during such a serious

The Reunion

A woman stares at the
first U.S. blacks she
has ever seen.

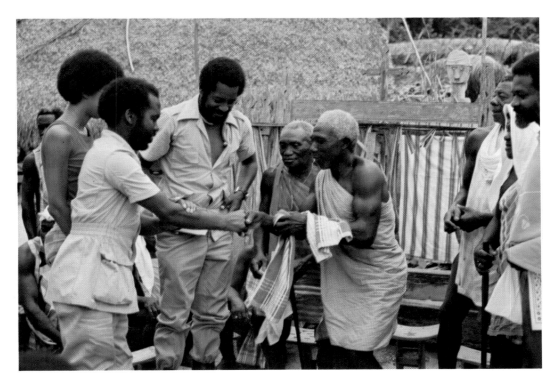

The chieftain
welcomes Counter
and Evans.

A native drummer calls
villagers together to
celebrate.

Acrobat dances while balancing on *kulu* sticks.

The whole village dances.

discourse. Our interpreter translated the chief's remarks as, "If you are part of us, and we have the same ancestors, then why have you not heard of us, and are you still *bakrah schlaffra* (white man's slaves)?"

The second question hit us like a thunderbolt. We were stunned beyond words. The villagers stared at us intently waiting for a response. We looked at each other with disbelief, yet we knew that these people had never heard of us. After all, those Surinam slaves who had not escaped into the bush with the freedom fighters had remained as slaves on the large plantations near the coastal cities until the emancipation proclamation. What was to keep them from thinking that we might still be in bondage? It was years before we admitted to each other that the question had brought tears to our eyes. At the same time, we had tried to hide them from each other.

We learned later that the Bush Afro-Americans are extremely knowledgeable and proud of their own history, which they have passed down through oral tradition and dance. They will quickly say that they are free Africans and "never had been *bakrah schlaffra.*"

We both responded to our *bahjah* that he should tell the chieftain that "we are not slaves in our land. Well, not really in the true sense of the word."

The headman then asked, "Well, have you won your fight?"

As we looked at him and the others around him, we were again reminded that these people were indeed fighters. Their ancestors had fought a guerrilla war for over one hundred years and won the right to recreate their old Africa in their new world, to live free of European domination. We responded by saying that "the battle was still being fought."

The headman seemed pleased with our answer. He then leaned over to speak to two older men and one older woman on the council. We began to feel some tension, a straining in our interaction, and the atmosphere became more serious. The chieftain sat erect on his *bangi,* examined our faces carefully, and asked us in a probing voice (the entire group of villagers staring silently at us), "Then have you found the road home?" This confused us. What did he mean? We asked our interpreter, the headman, and a few of our boatmen who were standing nearby.

The Reunion

One of the older men in the group explained that the ancestors of these people and now they themselves felt that "their forebears were stolen from their homelands by *bakrah* people with guns, taken to the ocean by a ship, and sailed around and around in a huge circle for many days so that they would be disoriented. After this ordeal they were then deposited in another part of Africa as slaves, to work like animals on land taken by the white man. Many escaped the slave plantations or large ships when they landed in the ports, and they fled into the deep rain forest thinking that they were still in Africa," indeed, not a far-off land like South America.

Such belief is not surprising: both the wild flora and fauna of Surinam and French Guiana are very similar to that of West Africa. Many species of plants and animals seem to have almost exact analogs on the two continents. Searching for a road leading back home to their African nations, and failing to find their homelands within the hundreds of miles they explored in the dense forests of Dutch and French Guiana, these people had recreated a "little Africa" in the deepest and almost inaccessible jungles of South America.

Counter asked our *bahjah* to tell the headman and the entire village that "we are in fact also searching for the road home. And this bush nation is a very important stop along that road back to our mutual ancestral homeland. You are the connecting link between the African-Americans like ourselves in the United States and our brothers and sisters in Africa." Hearing this, the men and women around us began to clap their hands crosswise and in a rhythmic fashion. This, we learned, signifies approval.

Evans told the *bahjah,* "Tell the headman and the villagers that we have a poem which expresses our feelings." He recited it very slowly, so that everyone would have time to absorb it as it was translated: "I sought my friend and my friend forsook me. I sought my God and my God eluded me. I sought my brother and found all three."

In a few minutes the villagers and leaders understood what we had said to them. They were now visibly affected, shaken, and joyful. Some of the older women began to cry. They were saying, "*Gan Gadu* (heavenly Father) oh *Gan Gadu*, they are our people."

The Reunion

The women came forward to touch us; some put their arms around us to hug us tightly, saying *"ba"* (my brother); the men stood and extended their hands. They shook our hands in the conventional Western fashion but put their left hand under the right elbow while shaking with their right hand. This is considered a high tribute. It was like a big family reunion—a 350-year reunion between two long-separated Afro-American groups. Some of the women handed us their babies and smiled as we held them. We hugged and caressed the children with all the warmth and affection that we felt at that moment.

Almost a hundred men, women, and children gathered around us and expressed their pleasure at having us visit their land. Some brought us coconuts, others brought sugar cane, wild pineapples, and other gifts. Several families asked that we stay in their huts. We were moved to tears. The chieftain and council of elders seemed very pleased with the excitement and pleasure we had brought to their village and permitted the mild celebration to continue for about a half-hour.

Finally the chieftain asked everyone to be seated. There were still more formal matters to be considered. When we took our seats, he took a large drinking vessel, pottery of the type that is bartered from the indigenous Indians, and began to pour libations on the ground in the center of the *krutu* circle as he chanted a prayer. He passed the bottle to all the elders in the group, men and women. They each poured a few drops on the ground, chanted a brief prayer, then poured some of the liquid in a calabash gourd and drank it down in one gulp. The bottle was finally passed to us. Counter poured a small amount on the ground, reciting a prayer, which was translated for the villagers: "O God, I humbly beseech you to shed your blessings on the people of this village and let us live to get back to the United States to tell our brothers and sisters about this beautiful find, this magnificent revelation. Our mission is a moral one; help us to keep our purpose in mind and guide us safely in our efforts." He drank from the gourd and coughed loudly, convulsing as he swallowed. The native palm alcohol must have been over 100 proof, so strong that the natives inevitably frowned as they drank it.

The Reunion

The bottle was passed to Evans, and he also recited a prayer as he poured a libation on the ground: "Lord, please guide us safely in this world with which we are so unfamiliar and help us to grow in wisdom as we go about our appointed tasks." Evans drank liberally from the gourd, only to grunt loudly and grimace as the hot liquid went down. He found it almost too strong for human consumption. The people were tickled by our obvious lack of experience with such a strong drink, laughing loudly at our attempts to swallow the harsh liquid.

The chieftain spoke to us through his *bahjah,* as if reciting a benediction. Our *bahjah* interpreted:

The chieftain says that he and his people welcome you to their nation. He is proud that you would choose their land for your visit. They have never heard of this place from which you come. They did not know that some of our people had been lost in this place. You are the first black African people to visit us from your land and they are proud to have you. You may enter our land and live here as long as you wish. You must obey our rules and respect our people, and especially follow the advice of the older ones. We hope that you will learn from us about our lives here on the rivers. We are people of the river as well as people of the bush. We hope to learn about you also. We only ask that when you go back to your land you will teach what you have learned from us to the African people there, if it is worth that—and we thank you very much. *Gan tanee* [we are most grateful].

We stood and shook hands again, this time with the entire council and many of the tribal members standing nearby. By now the crowd had grown much larger. The elders passed us some spirits, and several men brought us freshly cut coconuts filled with cool, natural juice. We could see drums being brought in from nearby huts. Some were the extremely large *agheeda* drums which are about six feet tall and about three feet in diameter. Others were the smaller *apenti* drums. The crowd rushed forth to touch us, hug us, shake our hands. The entire village seemed to come alive with laughter and good cheer. Then a large, powerful Afro-American man of about thirty, dressed in a colorful toga, started to beat out a syncopated rhythm on the *agheeda* drum while chanting an African song. Others joined in as the entire village welcomed their brothers from the United States.

Then two more very muscular young men came forward in the center of the crowd carrying two long thick poles. The

The Reunion

group began to chant loudly and rhythmically as a third man leapt astride the two poles and began the most incredible dance we had ever seen. As the two men holding the ends of the poles at waist level slammed them together and then pulled them apart, the dancer twisted and jumped from pole to pole to the beat of the music without losing his balance. The women sang and clapped their hands. We joined in by clapping our hands and dancing in the central circle. Everyone, men, women, and children, laughed at the two black strangers attempting to dance to their music. Realizing we were amusing our hosts, we began to dance more vigorously, using some of the latest American soul steps. We finally asked two of the young women standing nearby to join us in the center of the circle and dance with us. They reluctantly and shyly accepted and then began one of their vigorous bush dances. The enthusiasm, laughter, and good will of the crowd was something to behold. The whole village rocked like a black rhythm and blues concert.

We were to learn that music is a natural part of the bush people's lives. Singing is their most common form of music, and everyone sings. They even sing their daily greetings. It is said of the bush people that some are great singers but everyone is a good singer. Their singing is very African in its intonation and beat. Their songs are generally about their loved ones, about some romance between a man and a woman, or the beauties of nature.

The women's voices are mezzo-soprano by our standards and are modulated to sound like musical instruments. The chorus is common among the women, the most rhythmic songs accompanied by hand claps, in which the hands are cupped for a fuller sound.

The major musical instrument is the hand drum. There are several kinds of drums among the Bush Afro-Americans, most of which can be traced directly back to Africa. The *apenti* drum, most frequently used for dance ceremonies and signal communication, is similar to a drum used for the same purpose throughout West Africa. The large *agheeda* drum, on the other hand, seems to have originated in the Surinam bush. A small drum used for communication, called a talking drum, is a West African survival.

Fortunately Stedman had drawn pictures of a collection of musical instruments used by the slaves and bush freedom fighters of his time, all models of the ones used by the Africans in their homeland. Many of these same instruments, the same wood-carved instruments, survive in the Surinam rain forest today. We recognized some of the musical instruments cataloged by Stedman in our introductory ceremony. For percussion, dried shells of nuts filled with seeds or pebbles are tied around the women's ankles, creating a maraca rattle when the women dance. These anklets are very similar to those worn in many West African countries for the same purpose.

Music and dance are usually communal affairs. People sing or dance solos on occasion, but usually with backup singers or a chorus. To lift the spirits, for holy matters, good wishes for a traveler, the birth of a child—all these are occasions for song and dance. Perhaps in this way more than any other American blacks have held on to their African traditions. Their music and dance can be traced directly back to the early African slaves.

The bush people asked us to sing and play some of our music for them on the drums. We sang some spirituals and rhythm and blues songs for them. They seemed to enjoy the songs, keeping time with the music and humming along with songs they had never heard. They seemed to feel the emotional power of the songs, especially the spirituals.

We were struck by the way the bush people enjoyed our tape recordings. We played every kind of music for them, from Lightnin' Hopkins's "Jesus Won't You Come by Here" to Rachmaninoff's "Rhapsody on a Theme of Paganini." They showed a clear and marked preference for Afro-American soul music. Initially the villagers would stand quietly and listen to our tape recordings, but then they would gradually begin to dance. If we had to name the top six musicians, those whose music was most often requested, we would say Otis Redding, Lightnin' Hopkins, James Brown, Stevie Wonder, Aretha Franklin, and Mahalia Jackson. Drummers played along with the rhythm and the blues, and people danced to the music of James, Aretha, and Stevie as if it were their native music. They took their dancing as seriously as we do.

Everyone who heard the recorded songs of Paul Robeson thought that he must be a physical giant. They loved his voice and said that they imagined the tall *kan kan* tree singing when they heard his voice. They wanted to know about him: Was he from Africa also? How big was he? Was he a strong warrior? We explained that he was indeed a giant, and a strong warrior in many ways.

The day we were introduced to the village, we selected a few songs by Stevie Wonder, Otis Redding, James Brown, and Aretha Franklin and turned the recorder's volume up full blast. We moved back to the center of the circle and danced to a rocking tune by Stevie Wonder. The villagers looked on and listened curiously as we danced alone to this strange music. Several of the children entered the circle and started following our steps. This brought a great deal of approving laughter from the women who were still standing together. Gradually everyone began to sway back and forth to the beat of the soul music. Before long, most of the village was jumping, rocking, and doing their steps to our American soul music, precisely in step with the beat. Evans joked, "It's genetic." It was like a powerful spiritual celebration at the proverbial "sugar shack"—we continued to "party" until late afternoon.

To look at the Bush Afro-Americans of Surinam is to see Africa. To listen to them is to hear the music and languages of Africa. We wondered just how West Africans would react to seeing the Surinam bush people, who had held on to their ancient traditions better than most nations on the African continent today.

The fun and frolic were halted when the chieftain walked into the center of the crowd, waved his hand, and politely asked us to follow him and the accompanying elders back down to the river. The crowd, still jubilant, followed us down a path toward the river. But the elders looked stern and serious and would not smile. We were nervous about the sudden shift in their attitude, their grim expressions. Where were they taking us? Had we offended them in some way? Why did they look so serious? We then looked at each other for comfort. These were our brothers and sisters; we were in their hands and trusted them implicitly. But we still felt uncomfortable. As we reached the river, the elders raised their hands and asked the villagers to halt. The chieftain beckoned us to join him in a small hut. Our interpreter was as puzzled as we were but said, "I think they have some kind of spiritual ritual for you to participate in—they are taking you into the medicine man's hut."

The Reunion

The house we were entering was indeed a rather unusual
looking thatched roof hut. There was a man standing near a
small shrine in front of the hut, beating softly and slowly on
a long *agheeda* drum. Each of four poles around the hut had
skulls of wild pigs or tapirs mounted on them. Small cloth
banners were hung on stakes in front of this dwelling. We
smiled at the drummer as we followed the chieftain into the
hut, but he did not return the smile. Our interpreter joined
us. Once inside, we were asked to remove all our clothing.
We were quite surprised. Was this to be a manhood ritual?
Would they parade us through the village naked? We had
seen several naked young boys and girls in the village, but
all young people from the stage of puberty and all adults
were wearing a loincloth called a *pangi.*

The chieftain introduced us to the head medicine man and
high priest, Apauti, a powerful-looking and well-preserved
man of fifty-seven. He was covered with a white clay or powder that gave him a ghostly appearance. They told our interpreter that once our clothes were off, we were to put on the
strips of bright cloth they had placed on two large, beautifully carved wooden stools in front of us. The medicine man
said that we had to have our bodies and souls washed; we
were to have clean souls and good spirits to live among the
people of this village. They stepped outside the hut and
waited for us to change our clothes. They had indicated an
acceptance of us outsiders as brothers, but we were not
members of their nation and had to prove ourselves and our
good intentions. We understood their caution and respected
them for their attempts to protect their village. We hurriedly
stripped off our clothes and donned our first *pangis.* We had
come here to visit, to study, not to take up permanent resi-
dence and adopt all of their customs, but we would learn
nothing about the intricacies and nuances of their culture
without participating in their essential, sacred rituals.

We stepped out of the hut amid smiles and chants of approval from the villagers who were now standing in front of
the hut. *"Moi, moi"* (beautiful, beautiful), the smiling villagers were saying. The men began shaking our hands and
shoulders to give us courage. As the onlookers stood on the
banks, Apauti hurriedly ushered us down to the river and
asked us to wade in. Once we were in the river, he told us to
stand still in the shallow water. He walked back up to the

The Reunion

river bank and in front of the entire village chanted a long and moving prayer. We could not understand the language but felt the spirit and warmth of its cries, chants, and moans as he spoke to God in our behalf. Many of the villagers who stood watching us from the bank joined in the ceremony. The scene was reminiscent of baptisms conducted at black churches, scenes we had known growing up in the South, the kind that must have been conducted in Africa long before Christianity reached its shores. Our interpreter tape-recorded the entire ritual and much later, through careful interpretation by specialists, we learned that in one segment of Apauti's long prayer he said,

Oh God whom we have known since Kumassi. O great Kad-yamon, Kadyampon. I beg you to bless and protect these our African brothers from another land. They have come from far away. You have guided them to us safely. They have been looking for us and they have found us. . . . It is possible that we are all from the same mother in Africa. . . . They are our African brothers and they will show us the road home.

How did the medicine man Apauti, who had never set foot in Africa, know of Kumassi, the ancient capital of Ghana? "Kadyamon, Kadyampon," literally interpreted, means, "The unchanging One whom I can lean on and He will never fail me." It is the precise interpretation of the Ghanaian, "Twete a mon Twete om pon." We know that many of the enslaved Africans brought to Surinam were from what was called at that time the Guinea Coast, which includes Ghana and several other West African countries. Many came from Guinea proper, Togo, Dahomey (Benin), Angola, and other parts of Africa. Yet many aspects of the Ghanaian cultures seem to have emerged as dominant.

Following his prayer, Apauti walked into the water to us and sprinkled our bodies with a white clay called *pemba dot-tee* chanting prayers to the gods on our behalf. When our faces and bodies were smeared with the white substance, he requested that we move from the shallow to the slightly deeper waters and immerse our entire bodies. We were alarmed because we knew this river was filled with piranha, but reluctantly we backed into the deeper water. Evans was cautious, kneeling slowly but not immersing his body and head so Apauti grabbed his head and pushed him under. Then the medicine man asked us both to rise as he dipped two thick batches of fresh green leaves into the waters and

The Reunion

Medicine man, Apauti,
prepares to cleanse
Counter and Evans by
baptizing them before
they enter village.

The baptismal
ceremony.

The blessing.

then raised them to the level of our heads and shoulders to wash us. The crowd on the bank began to sing and chant refrains to the medicine man's prayers. Now the ritual really seemed like an old time southern baptism, but more haunting, more primitive.

"I am washing your bodies, your souls, our African brothers," Apauti chanted. "I am making you clean to walk among our people. We are the River People. We are African people. You are African people. You have been searching for us, and you have found us. Wash clean, wash deep, oh, wash clean." He shook the wet leaves at us and poured the water over our heads, as the crowd of onlookers on the bank chanted loudly.

Some of them ran into the water to join the sacred ritual. One woman ran into the river screaming and crying as she leaped between us, throwing herself at the foot of the medicine man and asking him to bless and cleanse her. She stayed in the water with us for much of the ceremonial washing. When Apauti said "kneel," she would direct us by pushing us to our knees, then joins us by kneeling herself and chanting the prayer refrains. A child of about six or seven also broke away from the crowd and charged into the water to join us. The crowd now raised their hands and chanted in a loud eerie sound that sounded like the wind rushing through trees: *wooo, eeeee.* Apauti raised the leafy bundles over his head and shouted toward the sky, "Kadyamon, Kadyampon. . . ." By now he loomed so powerful to us that we expected to hear thunder and see lightning at any moment.

Suddenly everything fell silent. Apauti walked around behind us and asked us to turn and face the river. We turned, and he, in a most eloquent gesture, dipped the two bundles of wet leaves into the river, raised them dripping water, and shook them above our heads one last time. Without looking behind him, he tossed the holy leaves over his shoulders into the flowing river stream. The bundles of leaves slowly floated away down the river. Whatever was evil or unacceptable in us, he had put it behind him and us. He beckoned us to step out of the water to the river's edge. There he picked up a short, elegantly carved wooden stick decorated with feathers and cowrie shells and a large round gourd mounted

The Reunion

on a stick and decorated with small inlaid stones. He touched both of us with the feathers and chanted more prayers for several minutes. Then Apauti stopped the ceremony abruptly and pronounced us "good spirits." He embraced each of us, then turned and departed quietly. We were now among the clean, the blessed, the touched, and could freely enter and move about the village.

"Moi, moi, me ba, me ba" (beautiful, beautiful, my brother, my brother), the crowd chanted as we left the river and headed back to the medicine man's hut to retrieve our clothes. People came forth to greet us again and touch us. The women again handed us their babies, and little children grabbed our hands. We had a sense of spiritual cleanliness of a kind we had not experienced since our childhood baptisms—a sense of family, a sense of holiness. We both had religious backgrounds, but in many ways these past few moments had been more like being in touch with God than any previous religious experience.

We arrived at the medicine man's hut with a large entourage. We changed into our Western clothes and started for our campsite. When we came out of the hut, the chieftain and medicine man greeted us with warm smiles and told us, through our interpreter, that some of the men would show us to a grass hut (called an *oso*), which they would let us use during our stay in the bush. They said that they knew we must be tired and in need of rest and that the village would become silent shortly after first darkness and not active again until the first sign of sunlight.

We were reluctant to accept the invitation to sleep in grass huts. We had brought along two large tents, complete with vital mosquito netting, for ourselves, our translator, and our technical equipment. The mosquitos in this area are carriers of yellow fever, malaria, and cause the disfiguring disease, filariasis. Snakes, tarantulas, and large rats are frequent companions in huts. We found that the bush people deal with this problem by sleeping in hammocks strung on the large poles within the huts. Their hammocks, some traded to them by the indigenous Amerindians, are hung from three to five feet above the ground and out of the range of most crawling pests and predators. We struck a compromise between ourselves and decided to live in the huts that our hospitable hosts had provided but erect our tents anyway in order to house our equipment, supplies, and assistants. If we found the huts unbearable despite our insect repellent, after a few days we would humbly request our hosts to let us move into our own *oso.*

The villagers found our brightly colored (green and orange) tents appealing. We had chosen those colors so that in case we were ever lost in the dense jungle we could climb to the top of the tall foliage and lay the contrasting bright hues on top of the trees to be spotted by search planes. The foliage is so thick and tall (about fifty to one-hundred feet high in most places) that one can be spotted from the air by no other means. We pitched the tents in a space selected for us by the village elders while a small audience looked on curiously. They were obviously unfamiliar with tents and were fascinated with an *oso* that came out of a bag and could be erected in about twenty minutes. Men and women wanted to enter, to explore the walls and windows. They were especially fond of the mosquito netting built into the tent when its purpose was explained to them. We stored our equipment, food, and other supplies. By then darkness had arrived and the natives quietly wandered back to their homes, no doubt to contemplate us and our surprising visit. We headed to our hut with a lantern, a tape recorder, and pads on which to record the day's events before we fell asleep. We had so much to analyze, so much to write about.

The Reunion

The Bush Family   The villagers rise with the sun. We were usually awakened by the chorus of domestic cocks crowing throughout the village and the singing of the birds. Chores are begun early, around 6:00 A.M., because there are only about thirteen hours of sunlight for doing chores, hunting, and planting, and sunlight is the only light in the remote rain forest.

The morning begins with communal or individual washing at the river banks. Children up to the age of puberty bathe nude, but adults cover themselves with cloth until their lower bodies are immersed. Following the morning bath there is a light breakfast of cassava bread and water and sometimes coconut juice. Frequently rice and leftover meats from the previous evening's meal are mixed and eaten as a morning meal. People eat when they are hungry rather than at prescribed times during daylight hours, and family meals are eaten in the early evenings.

As we emerged from our hut in the mornings, we were generally met by children. The children typically were less inhibited about showing their curiosity than were the young and old adults. We took our baths in our assigned place in the river, which had a cool, fast-moving stream of shallow water. As outsiders, even after weeks in the village, we were not permitted to bathe near the women.

The villages of this area are always situated about five meters higher than the river level for several reasons: to prevent flooding when the river rises after heavy rains, to prevent flash flooding during tropical storms, and to ensure that daily rains will clean the village and wash organic debris downhill and into the river. A series of intricate trenches dug by experienced members of the village community allow the rainwater to drain off into the river. The curves and corners of each trench looked as if they had been designed by modern civil engineers. A series of paths through the thick bush lead to the river. At the end of each path, magnificently carved family canoes are tied up by dried vines to wooden spikes sunk deep in the ground. When we wanted to bathe, we simply moved the boats and waded into the water. Children always joined us, laughing and splashing and watching us as we lathered with soap and brushed our teeth in the cool fast streams.

After morning baths we generally prepared a breakfast of canned foods while the children looked on. A few older chil-

The Reunion

Women tending
cassava gardens.

dren and some adults would join the crowd, watching our every move. If we gestured to offer them some of our canned ham and crackers, they usually refused, laughing. A few of the children, gradually drawn by curiosity to accept a bite, were laughed at by the other children. When all would gather around to examine the food, some were repelled by the smell. Others just stared at it and refused to accept any. But the children found our wafer biscuits quite acceptable.

Pokaytee is a large village connecting several smaller villages, its red clay earth reminiscent of Georgia or Alabama. Walking through the village was like walking in a remote African village of an earlier era. The organization and activities of the village had changed little in two centuries. Arranged in a crescent around a central clearing were beautifully painted, natural wood thatched huts. Men and women busily go about their daily chores, the men to some spot in the outlying forest to hunt game or to their canoes to fish. Many women head off to the deep forest to harvest their rice. Some of the older women attend smaller plots of manioc cassava (a potatolike starch source that is a staple) and peanuts cultivated near their huts. Women clean their huts and sweep the bare earth around the hut. For a broom the thick natural flowering part of the palm tree is used, and for a dust pan they use the large fan-shaped leaf of the palm tree. The village is immaculate, the huts impeccably clean. Several of the men considered too old to travel long distances to clear thick forest areas for the planting of crops weave large palm fronds for the roofs of houses. Children assist parents in all tasks, watching and learning new ones. Little girls pound rice with large wooden sticks called *mata tiki.* Little boys run errands, go fishing, and shoot birds with their slingshots.

Everyone greeted us as we wandered throughout the village, and we occasionally stopped to talk to some of those involved in tasks we were not familiar with. The greetings had a warm musical quality. Hello is a cheerful *"Dah."* "How are you this morning?" is sung *"Dah wikki ba,"* which literally means "Hello; are you up and alert, brother?" The answer to this greeting is an equally melodious phrase, *"Wikki ooooh."* Learning a little of their language by ear and analyzing the sounds phonetically, we began to exchange greetings in their tongue. This effort was met with amused smiles, sometimes

The Reunion

Villager sews calf band on bottles and sticks.

Seventy-year-old sews palm fronds for the roof of his hut.

shy laughter. But in every case the people answered our attempts with a beautiful chant.

All day long the people go about their appointed tasks. Many carry wooden objects or baskets of food on their heads as they move about the village. Some carry children on their backs as they work. Between chores some of the young women braid each other's hair and chat in the shade of a large tree. Most of the villagers waited until we greeted them before they looked up to acknowledge our presence.

One day while visiting the far side of the village, we met a woman who was mixing the hot pepper, cayenne. When we asked her about the tear-evoking substance she was pounding with mortar and pestle, she said that she would use parts of it as spice and burn the rest inside her hut with the door closed in order to expel insects and rodents. The smoke from burning pepper is a potent pesticide, which leaves a lasting film inside the hut. She offered us a large portion of the ground hot peppers to use in our food. Cayenne pepper has been used as a spice and for other purposes since the days of Stedman.

The people were generous and kind to their new guests, eager to show us hospitality. Some invited us into their huts and offered us food, coconut water, and their blessings. Such encounters, touching and meaningful to us, were like visiting families and friends in the rural South. There was not much material wealth to share, but what there was they shared graciously. Stedman had described this remarkable sense of community and generosity when he said of their forebears, "I however think they are a happy people, and possess so much friendship for one another, that they need not be told to 'love their neighbor as themselves'; since the poorest negro, having only an egg, scorns to eat it alone; but were a dozen present, and every one a stranger, he would cut or break it into just as many shares."

We spent a few weeks in Pokaytee and villages nearby observing the culture and recording its sounds. Almost everyone had something new to teach us: men, women, children, all had special roles within the family and the community.

Each family is largely responsible for providing for itself, to hunt, fish, plant, harvest, and build dwellings and boats. Some tasks are done communally. When large animals, such

The Reunion

Bush women braid
Counter's hair.

Evans sports a braided
hair style.

as tapirs, are killed for food, the meat is shared by the hunter's family with other families and older women and men of the village who are incapable of gathering food themselves.

The structure of today's Bush Afro-American family has its origins in the early escaped slave societies. As Stedman indicated, monogamy among the slaves was common. Polygamy also existed in some instances, depending on the background of the Africans involved.

When the enslaved Africans escaped into the bush country, the entire family structure was reorganized. For example, more men escaped to the rain forest than women, and with fewer women an unusual family structure evolved. According to the elders, some of the first families were made up of a woman, her several husbands, and their children. The continuous one-hundred-year war between the Bush Afro-American freedom fighters and their former enslavers had a profound effect on the family. Husbands were killed, leaving behind wives and children. Women warriors were killed, leaving behind husbands and children. Widowed women were invariably taken into other households and widowed husbands generally remarried. Families were raised on the run because of the relentless pursuit of European mercenaries and soldiers during wars. As soon as one bush village was discovered by the soldiers, the natives had to relocate.

In some instances entire slave populations from a single plantation escaped at one time or over a period of months or years. Having lived together as a captive unit on the same compound for years, the population was a closely knit unit in which many people were interrelated biologically and socially. It is logical, then, that when an entire slave population of a single plantation escaped to the bush interior they would remain together as a single unit or clan. Today in the Surinam bush the descendants of such clans still bear the name of the slave plantation from which their ancestors escaped. One group told us that they were the *"misi John lo"* (their word *lo* means clan), which means that they descended from the group who escaped the Johns plantation. Besides plantation names, some clans reflected the name of the ethnic group that enslaved them and from whom they

The Reunion

escaped. These names were not preserved for reasons of pride but merely as a form of identification. Studying early Dutch slavery documents in The Hague, we found that many of these names were traceable back over hundreds of years to the former white enslaver.

Each clan is broken down into extended families, each family a single but interconnected unit. The Bush Afro-American families can vary in their makeup from the usual nuclear family, consisting of father, mother, and children, to polygamous units. Grandparents are integral to most families, serving as advisers to their children and surrogate parents to their grandchildren.

The oldest male brother of a woman may have more to do with the raising of her sons than does her husband. Uncles are very important in family life because, although they are emotionally involved with their sisters' children, it is said that there is enough distance to assure objectivity in helping to rear them. Fathers, they believe, are too emotionally involved with a child's development, which can mean bad family relations.

All families and clans are matrilineal, meaning that everything is passed down in the female line of the family, including children and material goods. This arrangement of a kinship based on the mother's lineage originated in both West African matrilineal societies and in the organization of the first escaped slave societies.

While each family provides for many of its own needs, in raising major crops the entire clan shares in the work. Clans may own plots of land that they themselves have cleared and planted where they and they alone grow crops. Poachers are punished or run off this land. Land ownership is understood to be the right to work the land, not to own it in a Western sense.

Interclan marriage is respectable, but intrafamily marriage is absolutely forbidden. Incest is considered one of the worst crimes and sins in the bush and may draw extreme punishment, even a death penalty, for the adult perpetrator. Interclan marriage brings many gifts to the families involved.

As in other cultures, families gather together in times of celebration and mourning. Entire families celebrate births, successful hunting trips, and good harvests. Families and

The Reunion

Husband and wife.

A typical nuclear
family.

Husband and wife
traveling in canoe.

clans mourn dead family members at funerals. The most striking thing about the family structures is that no one is excluded—no man, woman, or child is without a family. Perhaps it is their long history of struggle for survival against outside forces that has led to their sense of togetherness. Their black relatives in the United States, who had strong family bonds for a short time following the period of slavery, have seen those ties fade and weaken. We felt the loss of such bonds most poignantly in experiencing the bush people's care for each person and every family.

The men see themselves as the heirs and guardians of a precious, delicate freedom, which has been constantly threatened since their earliest ancestors fled slavery more than three centuries ago. An awareness of impending danger pervades their culture and has molded within them a special sense of urgency, affecting all aspects of their existence. A man is expected to be more than a protector and provider; he must communicate the spirit of the fighting ancestors to the next generation. Their sacrifices, their suffering, their bravery, discipline, pride, and ultimate victory over the slaveholders are made part of a child's everyday life.

Roles defined for the men of the village, such as that of hunter, woodsman, and house builder, are similar to those found in Western societies. There are other roles quite different from those of Westerners. It takes time, patience, and a good deal of luck on the part of the outsider to witness, for example, a man teaching the elder sons of his sisters what society expects of them as they mature. Men, specifically the *liree,* or village historian, maintain the culture orally, reciting historical facts and stories to the villagers that both entertain and enlighten. Although the Bush Afro-Americans do not have a written language as such, they do have a series of markings that communicate messages.

The Bush Afro-American men have a heritage of strength and defiance. Young men are instructed about the ways their forebears survived the torture of the slaveholder and the horrors of slavery when lesser men would have died to extinction. European observers wrote about the hell and terror endured by the male slaves who attempted to break out of bondage and fight for their freedom. None stated it more movingly than Stedman:

The Reunion

What good man can reflect the tear-stain'd eye
When blood attest even slaves for freedom die?
On cruel gibbets, high disclos'd they rest,
And scarce one grown escapes one bloated breast.
Here sable Caesar feel the Christian rod,
There Afric Platos, tortur'd hope a God,
While jetty Brutus for his country sighs,
And sooty Cato with his freedom dies!

Stedman went on to point out that "the above names, with
such as *Nero, Pluto, Charon, Cerberus, Proserpine, Medusa,*
etc., are usually given to negro slaves, in exchange for
Quacco, Quacy, Quamy, Quamina, Quasiba, Adjuba, etc."
These are Ghanaian day names still in use today in Africa
and Surinam. Quacoo is the day name of a male child born
on Wednesday, Quacy, a male child born on Sunday, and
Quamy (or Kwame), a male child born on Saturday (the late
Kwame Nkrumah of Ghana).

With the bush people we had to be patient observers, not
avid questioners. What questions we did ask required careful
diplomacy. We learned very early that if the bush dwellers
do not feel pressured by prying questions or made uncomfortable by behavior that smacks of snooping, they can be
warmly open and informative. We made a conscious decision not to disturb their relaxed life-style with badgering
questions. We knew from what our interpreter could tell us
that they are not high-strung, will not allow their daily pace
to be rushed, do not take well to anyone who is tense and
disruptive to their way of life.

For something more than brief and evasive responses, one
waits until the people are ready to offer them. The wait is
sometimes long for a discussion of a particular aspect of
their culture.

The history, religion, and philosophy of the bush people
are vibrant and intermingled. It seems that little in the culture is unrelated to these three elements. A direct or abrupt
inquiry about the cultural, historical or philosophical significance of an event or an object is likely to be ignored or responded to with feigned ignorance. To indirect, diplomatic,
and unthreatening queries the answers can be elaborate and
revealing.

Probably our best illustration of what is expected of men
was observed almost by chance. The event that attracted our
attention and eventually led to the detailed description of the
men's role primarily involved boys.

The Reunion

78

A village leader

A village *bahjah*.

A village *bahjah*.

A boat and drum
maker from Pokaytee.

One morning while climbing into one of the boats for a brief trip across the river to visit the relatives of the head-man, we saw a picturesque scene on one of the rocks out in the river. There, surrounded by several boys of eight to twelve, stood a man who appeared to be teaching the youngsters to fish with a bow and arrow. We asked the boat-men if they thought we would disturb the teacher or pupils if we paddled in closer. The response was "let's go and see."

We pulled in closer, stopped the boat, and explained that we only wanted to watch. If we were a disturbance, we would leave. The teacher invited us to stay, explaining that the boys had to learn to master the bow and arrow, distractions or no distractions.

It was a training session—they were not shooting at real fish. The teacher used a green, unbarked coconut as the practice target. The coconut was thrown into the rushing waters on the blind side of the boys. When it popped up, they were to shoot it with the five-foot-long arrows as if it were a fish.

In an hour and a half all but one of the boys showed some progress, the exception forgiven because he was two or three years younger than the others. The youngest continued to miss the target, becoming increasingly frustrated when the teacher bellowed at him. Finally he started to cry. The man dismissed the older boys and continued the lesson even more intensely, but without cruelty, with the younger lad. Each time the little fellow missed his mark, the teacher would take the bow and arrow himself, have one of the older boys throw the coconut into the water on his blind side, and shoot it when it came into view. All the while the young boy observed how the teacher stood with his bow and arrow at the ready, looking straight ahead, prepared for the target to come from either side, and, finally, swiftly shooting slightly ahead of the moving target. At long last the boy hit the target three out of five times, and the day's target-fishing session was over. We had become so involved that we felt as relieved as the boy.

The teacher, the older boys, and the young one gathered their bows, arrows, and paddles, climbed into their boat, and prepared to leave the rock. We asked the man if he would have a few minutes to talk after he took the boys back to the village. We wanted to follow them to their village in our

The Reunion

A family discusses the harvest plans.

Husband and wife leave family to travel up river.

Man teaches boys to
fish with bow and
arrow.

Village elder carries
palm fronds to help
build hut for young
couple.

boat. The teacher asked what would be the nature of our questions. They would only concern his methods of teaching the boys to fish with bow and arrow, we assured him. He looked a bit puzzled, but one of the boatmen who knew the teacher intervened on our behalf. The teacher calmed down but walked away from us toward the boys and the boat, telling the boys to leave without him. He returned to us and asked our interpreter "What is so important about teaching little boys to fish with bow and arrow that would attract the attention of grown men?"

We explained that in our culture it was rare that boys of eight to twelve were ever taught anything but games for playing and a few safe and simple tasks. Even then they were never taught as intensely as he had his pupils. They certainly would not be introduced to anything so potentially lethal as bows and five-foot arrows until they were teenagers.

His eyes moved slowly from one of us to the other with a look that seemed to say, "Are you kidding?" He turned to our interpreter, saying, "There is much difference in our two worlds, I see." What could have been a courteous way of ending the discussion was instead the gambit of a skilled raconteur.

He said that they started very early in preparing the boys for their roles in the community. The young boys of today, the men of tomorrow, are the protectors of tribal survival. Their environment is fraught with dangers and the future leaders have to be taught the importance of vigilance and agility of mind and body. One who is unskilled in the survival methods of the bush or unwary of its dangers invites destruction and death, not just for himself but for his family and, eventually, for his people.

We are people of the river more than the bush, therefore, we must master the river and teach the boys to do the same. First, a boy must be taught to paddle a boat. After this he must learn to use the *kulu* stick to push the big boats off the dangerous rocks in the river. When he is older, he must learn how to make a boat. He must learn how to fell a tree, drag it to the river, hew out the log to a depth that can be burned, then he must carefully burn the inside of the log, stretch it to the proper width, plane the sides with an axe to the correct thickness, and balance and finally decorate the boat.

The Reunion

Much of our food is the fish in the river and that is why we teach the boys to fish well. But we are not only fishermen; we are hunters and farmers too. A man is expected to be a good hunter, to help feed his family, and we start the boys early in becoming aware of the sights, signs, and sounds of the jungle. Just as the sight of a broken twig here and the faint smell of tobacco smoke there helped the rebel fathers evade and defeat the Dutch soldiers many years ago, so can a keen awareness of the subtleties of jungle animal behavior help a boy track the elusive agouti or avoid the deadly jaguar.

The tracking skills of the boys are so well developed that when we lost the small black rubber eyepiece that keeps light out of the rear of the camera, a lad of about twelve went back into the dark, leaf-strewn, muddy, overgrown jungle and found the eyepiece within forty-five minutes.

Farming is a major activity in the bush, and there are specific roles defined for the men in the clearing of the land. They cut down the large trees, let them dry for a while, then burn the cut trees and bushes. This done, the women plant and harvest the crops. Because of such physically demanding work as cutting down trees with axes, dragging the trees to the riverside, and paddling their boats, the bush men have extremely well-developed upper bodies. The barrel chest is commonplace among the men.

One important sign of manhood among the bush dwellers is the ability to bear pain without the expression of agony. This attribute is so significant that during certain ritual dances the men compete to see who can tolerate the greatest pain without flinching. The endurance of pain without crying out was mentioned by Stedman numerous times. One captured rebel was described by Stedman as "the most moderate and finest looking black that was perhaps ever seen," who refused to acquiesce to the threats of his former white enslaver although he [the rebel] was looking into the face of death.

[the enslaver:] ". . . the *torture* this moment shall make you confess crimes as black as yourself as well as those of your hateful accomplices." To which the negro, who now swelled in every vein with indignation and ineffable contempt, said, "Massera, the tigers have trembled for these hands," holding them up; "and dare you think to threaten me with your wretched instruments? No, I despise the utmost tortures you can now invent, as much as I do the pitiful wretch who is going to inflict them." Saying which, he threw himself down on the rack, where, amidst the most excruciating torments,

The Reunion

Making rope.

Cutting small trees.

Sawing logs.

he remained with a smile, without uttering a syllable; nor did he ever speak again, until he ended his unhappy days at the gallows.

Although the men spend a great deal of their time fighting the hostile rain forest for their basic livelihood, there is also a relaxed, humane side to them. Nowhere is this better reflected than in the wood carving, which they do well. This artistic skill is not the sole domain of a talented few who belong to special guilds as is customarily the case in African and Western societies; every man is expected to be a wood-carver. Of course, some are more talented than others, but wood carving is considered an essential skill and is the primary art form for the men of the bush nations.

Some of their handiwork is clearly African in origin, and other aspects probably originated in the Surinam bush. For example, their sitting stools and wooden combs are similar to those of West Africa, while some of the house designs and certain shrines clearly grew out of their Surinam experience.

The major resource of the bush nation, wood is the raw material for boats, paddles, combs, eating utensils, food paddles, food pounding boards, drums, and stools. Combining the utilitarian and the aesthetic in their crafts, the people have a saying that "nothing should be made unless it is beautiful." Young boys are taught to carve beautiful and intricate objects from a single piece of wood, and they refine their skill throughout their adult life.

The most common example of artwork is seen in their combs, elegantly carved structures with five to ten teeth, usually curved in their lower half and decorated with metal tacks and designs that carry different messages. Combs are carved by men and boys for the women they love and for themselves. We were often given combs by the women of the villages as gifts for us and "the women in our families."

Boat paddles are elegant, sometimes painted, and also generally carved by men for the women they love. Women's paddles, usually smaller than those of the men, are covered with sign messages. Children have diminutive paddles, which their fathers or uncles carve for them. Food paddles are smaller versions of boat paddles, with intricately designed necks or handles. They too are carved by the men for the women in their household.

The Reunion

Calabash dishes or gourds and a pot stirrer.

Religious statue protects the harvest.

Religious statue wards off evil spirits.

Combs carved from a
single piece of wood
or metal.

Typical stool, clothes
beater, and peanut
pounding board.

Pot stirrers and child's
pestle.

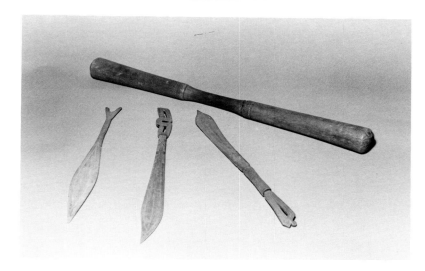

Stools, called *bangis,* are carved from single pieces of wood, and their designs can be traced directly back to West Africa. Some are crescent-shaped in the seat and legs and resemble those used by the Akan nation of Ghana. Others are rectangular in both seat and legs. Some have circular seats. The person who wants an uncommon stool creates a folding seat from a single strong piece of wood carved into separate boards, connected by wooden hinges and forming an X shape.

The simple mortars and pestles used in pulverizing foods, carved from extremely hard wood, are also works of art. Both instruments have smooth and subtle lines and are practically and aesthetically well balanced. They are carved by men for their mothers, wives, and daughters, and they are in use throughout the village from sunup to sundown. Circular trays two to three feet in diameter, used by the women to separate rice from the hull, are made from single pieces of wood richly decorated with intricate designs.

The men take special pleasure in carving drums. The most common drums are the tall *agheedas,* which are essentially six-foot cylinders with small wooden feet, and the large-belly *apenti* drums. The *agheeda,* usually painted, with few if any markings, is used in religious rites and other special ceremonies. Sometimes beaten with a small stick, it is more frequently beaten with the hand. The *apenti* drum, used in most of the ceremonial dances, can be covered with intricate designs and messages about the person who made it, and its natural wood is covered with brightly colored designs.

The women view themselves as guardians of the culture and, as one woman told us, the "springs of new life for the bush nation." In their erect bearing, devotion to their families, even in their shyness, they exude dignity, confidence, pride, beauty, and great inner strength. The women are dedicated and attentive mothers, but they participate fully in the day-to-day running of the village, from the small chores around their huts to the major decisions about village life. Women sit on the high councils, equal to the men, and occasionally a woman is appointed *bahjah* or head person of a village.

From our earlier observations of etchings made in the 1700s we could see that bush women had changed little in two hundred years. Their manner and style of dress, their

The Reunion

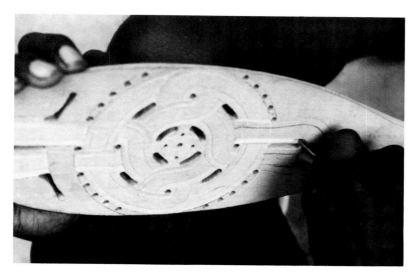

Carving paddle and
finished paddle.

Comb with metal tack decoration.

Paddles and boat prow found among the Aucaner people of the eastern Surinam rain forest.

An *apenti* drum.

method of carrying infants on their backs, their proud posture, their bundles balanced on their heads, all looked amazingly similar to the portraits of their distant ancestors. The role and position of the bush women of today can be viewed in the context of their history in Surinam.

Bush women are the bonds of the community and, indeed, the entire bush nation. Some of their names are Ahfee, Ahdieya, Abone, Ahmoyetia, Maymay, Samma, Bowu, Bodoba, Yodinna, Maishe, Poena, Osayeah, Oogeetee, and Ahmaiyo. Surviving in a rain forest requires diligent cooperation among husbands, wives, families, clans, and villages. The women have the responsibility for planting, harvesting, and preparing foods like dry rice, cassava bread, palm worm oil, and oil from nuts. Both women and men cook, but the men generally provide the meat proteins from hunting and fishing. The women are responsible for providing the children their knowledge of the culture and their general education. Mothers tend to spend more time with girls, while uncles and fathers teach and train young boys.

Realizing that we were not knowledgeable about the ways of the jungle, certain of the women adopted us as their *peekeen* (children; the term *peekeen* actually means small. *Peekeeneenee* means very small but has been used since Stedman's time to mean small child). And we were indeed like children in their jungle world. Such mentor adoption is apparently typical in "nonadvanced" cultures. Women of certain cultures will take outsiders into their households as helpless "infants" and teach them the methods of survival in their land. (The noted British anthropologist Colin Turnbull told us about a similar mother-child relationship he developed with a sympathetic woman in the Congo.) Our guardians provided us with essential information about the dangers of the bush and about their culture. They had many of the same concerns as women in other cultures: the proper rearing of their children, the family's health, their own marriage relationship, concern that their sons marry and be good providers.

The young women talk frequently about selecting a husband. When they are not working in the fields, transporting food by boat, or carrying out their many other daily tasks, they sit and talk while braiding each other's hair in a myriad of styles. Most young women, married between the ages of

The Reunion

Women sing and clap
to American music.

Village specialists
make metal anklets.

Seedshell anklets. Top,
Nigerian; bottom,
Surinam rain forest.

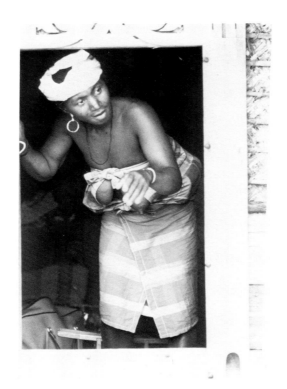

sixteen and nineteen, may freely select a mate, but parental approval is usually necessary. The male mate is generally older (in his late twenties), from another clan, and marries only because of his love for the woman. Monogamy is the traditional form of marriage among the bush villagers. Instances of polygamy were usually explained by a need to increase the number of children in a clan or to help work the fields and save a village. In those cases each wife had her own hut, built by her husband, and nearby cassava field, while the husband lived alone in a separate hut nearby.

The women serve as spiritual leaders, *obeah* women, in some villages. At funerals, the *obeah* woman (usually an older person) is asked by the family of the deceased to guard the spirits. We met women who practiced the *obeah* and who were in the process of removing evil spirits from a person suffering from some illness. These women were specially trained and highly regarded by the villagers. They seemed to possess a special charisma and had an aura of respectability. It is not unusual for the *obeah* woman to serve as the village midwife.

One afternoon during a visit to a neighboring village we observed a most unusual practice: a group of about fifty young women (and some of their children) had formed a circle around a single older woman. They were dressing the happy woman in colorful beads and cloth and singing to her. They paraded her through the village, chanting a beautiful chorus to her. As they passed several of the huts, other women came to their doors clapping their hands and joining in the passing chorus of song. The older woman and the singing women around her (which now formed a line on either side of her) walked throughout the entire village and ended their processional in the village center. After a few more songs and cheers and a brief dance from the delighted older woman, the group quietly disbanded and all went back to their respective huts, their soft laughter trailing as they slowly disappeared.

When we inquired about this ceremony, we were told that from time to time the young and middle-aged women of the village select an older woman who is single or widowed and pay her a special tribute by decorating her in bright colors, parading her throughout the villages, and singing songs to

The Reunion

Three generations of
one family in dugout.

Villagers sing to older
woman, "You are still
beautiful."

her that say she is still beautiful and still loved by the people of the village. These compassionate, so-called primitive people seemed in many ways so much more advanced than many of their counterparts in the United States.

We were amazed at how well the bush women had preserved their original African heritage. Many of the younger and older women decorate their faces and other parts of their bodies with skin marks (scarification), considered a sign of beauty by the women and men. They are also signs of pride, symbols of their African ancestors. We were told that many of the women arrange these scars in intricate designs on the usually covered parts of their bodies (like their buttocks, which they refer to as *gogo*) so that their husbands can feel them and derive pleasure as they make love in the dark.

The *moongas,* or leg bracelet, is another African retention of the bush women. These anklets are found today in back-country villages throughout West Africa, particularly among the traditional people of South East Angola. Skilled women make metal bracelets from any piece of scrap metal that they or their men can find. (We saw no evidence that metal of any kind is made by the Bush Afro-Americans. While the practice of making iron and other metals is common throughout West Africa, it seems not to have survived in Surinam.) The women of Surinam who specialize in this craft spend days pounding metal strips with a heavy metal rod or stone in order to shape the ring to fit a particular leg. A mother decorates her daughter with about ten rings on each leg; these anklets have a hairline separation and are removable at will. They are considered a sign of beauty and a symbol of their African ancestors and are passed down to a deserving young woman by an older relative or friend.

From the calabash gourd women carve dishes to be used as food utensils. The pulp is scooped out of the dried gourd, and the remaining bowl-shaped dish is decorated with the only carving we saw women do—a variety of designs that carry important messages to to the men they love. When a man has asked a woman for her hand in marriage, the potential bride may invite him to her hut and give him a drink of dark nectar from the calabash gourd with her women friends present. He drinks deep and finds her answer carved in the bottom of the gourd. In its more mundane use, the

The Reunion

109

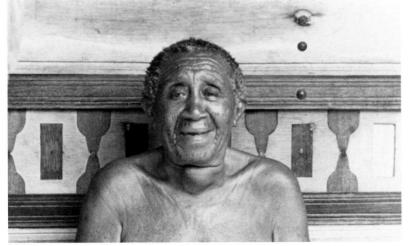

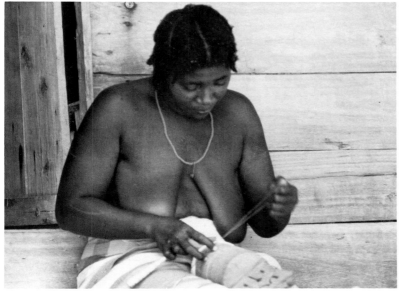

Woman sews calf band
on ancient wooden
block.

Young woman teaches
children to pound rice.

113

Woman wearing
necklace from suitor.

Young woman carries
baby sister.

gourd is a serving dish for rice or a rice and meat dish. A small crescent-shaped gourd, also decoratively carved on the inside, is used as a spoon or dip. Women make a variety of baskets, including cassava meal sifters, cassava squeezers, and bread mats, all retaining the natural brown color of the straw. Men and women both enjoy weaving natural straw fans.

A sight we shall forever cherish was that of a woman and child shooting dangerous rapids in a small wooden canoe. No concern was shown for the very fast streams, the large hidden boulders, or the deadly piranha in the water. A routine event for the bush women and men, to us it was awesome and frightening, and at the same time very beautiful.

The bush children are the treasure of their culture. Stedman commented admiringly on the love and concern the bush people have for their children. Infants are usually nursed and carried on their mothers' backs, West African style, for the first two years of life. Infants are also carried about on the backs of older girls of eight to fourteen while their mothers work in the fields. But children from infancy to about five years of age are near their mothers at all times. They roam in small groups throughout the village but never stray far from home without an adult.

As soon as girls are able to walk, they are taught to balance objects on their heads, a feat of grace and beauty and a valuable skill as well. But the males rarely carry things on their heads.

Girls of about five learn to paddle their mother's canoes, even through treacherous river rapids, showing no fear as they move through the swift cascades with increasing skill. At three to five, girls learn how to peel and prepare cassava. These youngsters develop great skill and dexterity in the use of large knives and machetes, particularly in chopping and then peeling sugar cane, the candy of the jungle.

Girls from age six to puberty assist their mothers in harvesting rice, using mortar and pestle (*mata tiki*) to pound the hull from the rice and in preparing cassava bread. The pestles used by these small girls can weigh from ten to twenty-five pounds, yet they work with them for long periods. This kind of activity develops great strength in the women. But parents are careful not to overtax children, telling them to rest in the shade after brief periods of labor. Adults usually

The Reunion

Young girl guides
grandmother through
rapids.

Learning to balance
objects.

Babysitting while
mother is in rice fields.

Carrying baby brother.

Typical eleven-year-old.

Typical twelve-year-old.

Watching boats arrive
from river bank.

Young girl blows
bubbles. A novelty in
the bush.

Walking along river.

Girls from the village
of Mainsi.

A brief rest from pounding rice.

work from sunup to sundown with a short rest period at midday, the hottest part of the day. Children work only a few hours a day and at tasks commensurate with their strength and development. For girls this usually involves food harvesting and preparation. They also perform many other chores around the hut and are required to observe the mother's work even when they are not helping.

When girls are not at work, they play like other children everywhere. Girls generally play with other girls. The play can involve such tasks as weaving baskets or braiding each other's hair in fancy styles. A few have wooden dolls carved by their fathers, and when they play with the dolls they imitate their mother's actions with younger siblings. They are taught the medicines used by women, and counting is taught by an older woman, usually a relative. Girls who show a special interest in plants may study with an *obeah* woman and become a medicine specialist. Some of these girls are selected by midwives to apprentice with them and learn their skills.

Boys from age five to puberty are required to assist their mothers in the heavier chores, such as removing weeds from around the hut or carving the heavy pestles for the women of their family to use in pounding rice. Young boys spend long afternoons fishing with string and hook on a pole or with special fishing traps. They garner lots of compliments and hugs as rewards for a good catch. The young boys are taught to hunt by older boys, an uncle, or their father.

In both the Bush Afro-American and the Indian settlements only the men hunt. It is rare to see a woman on a hunting trip. Both men and women indicated to us that the reason for this is that the animals often pick up the woman's scent, especially during periods of menstruation, from long distances. This, we were told, gives the game early warning and may attract dangerous animals like jaguars. We met an Indian woman who had been so attacked by a jaguar while on a hunting trip with her husband in the deep rain forest.

Typically a maternal uncle takes his nephew under his wing and teaches him the ways of the jungle. The main hunting tool is the wooden bow and bamboo arrows. Boys are taught to make bows and arrows, and they sometimes

The Reunion

Teaching cultural facts
to young girls.

receive them as gifts from relatives who trade with local Indian villages. This instrument can be used to shoot everything from fish to wild pigs and tapirs simply by changing the arrow tip.

We traveled with small boys through the bush to hunt for fish, the boys carrying specially designed harpoon-tipped arrows. When they came to a creek or side area of a river where fish are plentiful, they stole silently to the edge of the river, not cracking a twig underfoot. They took aim and fired the arrow into a large fish and seldom missed. When hunting for large game such as the wild pig (*pingo*), the young boys are usually accompanied by a much older boy or a male adult: the hunting grounds are often miles from the village, and jaguars are busy hunting for the same large game.

Very young boys are taught to carve in wood by an older male family member or by village specialists. They are proud of their skill and take pleasure in carving paddles and other objects for themselves, their friends, and their families. A young boy may carve a wooden comb for his sister or a paddle for his mother or a bow for his father. A father will carve a toy boat for his young son that is an exact replica of the large family canoe, and the boys play with such toys at the water's edge, as do children everywhere. Toy wooden guns carved by older male relatives are used to play games imitative of their historical war dances. A boy who is found to have a special penchant for wood carving is selected by the village specialist, and his skill is carefully cultivated so that it may be preserved in the village for generations to come.

Small boys who show exceptional verbal and learning skills are selected by some of the elders to become messengers, carrying news or questions to the leaders of other villages and carrying medicines from one village to another. Sometimes messengers travel long distances to summon *obeah* men for the sick or to describe the symptoms and bring back detailed messages to the medicine men about how to treat a certain condition.

Little boys who show a special interest in plants, often the children of *obeah* men, are sometimes selected to be trained as medicine men. All inhabitants of the bush must have a functional knowledge of the plants around them in order to

The Reunion

Fishing for minnows.

Waiting for boat ride.

Boy with toy boat
carved by his father.

Testing boat in river.

survive, but *obeah* men teach their young apprentices a superior knowledge.

Young boys learn from older ones the skills of paddling a dugout canoe through rapids on the large rivers. Like the young girls, boys are taught to negotiate dangerous rocks, heavy vegetation, and other aquatic obstacles. But only boys are taught to use the *kulu* stick, the ten-foot pole used in dangerous rapids to push the boat off rocks or to push it out of thick vegetation and shallow water.

When Apauti instructed his ten-year-old nephew in using a *kulu* stick to push a boat upstream in the rapids, he sat in the rear of the boat while the boy used the long pole from the front. Apauti stabilized the craft while the boy struggled to move the boat forward by pushing off the rocks with the *kulu* stick. They were pushed backward by strong rushing waters that splashed into the boat. The boy's wet body revealed powerfully muscled arms and frame as he struggled to keep the boat moving forward. His uncle Apauti shouted to him, "*kulu* stick right, *kulu* stick left, push harder, push harder." But his directions could not solve the dilemma: the rapids were stronger than the youngster struggling to steer the boat against them. Realizing that the boy was at the point of exhaustion, Apauti took his *kulu* stick and showed his nephew how to use it in fast waters. The boat began moving forward through the rapids under the strength of the man's powerful thrusts of the stick against the shallow rocks in the water. The young boy watched with admiration. His uncle complimented him for trying so hard and taught him a few new tricks about the proficient handling of the stick. The boy's lessons would extend a little longer each day, until he had mastered the *kulu* stick, a necessity for transportation in the rain forest.

Sometimes we joined a group of boys who walked through the bush at the edge of the village shooting birds with slingshots. These birds were defeathered, cleaned and roasted on sticks. The boys called these birds *sutti mofu,* or sweet taste. They always shared their *sutti mofu* with us and enjoyed watching us savor it. While we sat and ate with them, we'd ask them about the future and what they wanted to do when they became men. Many had no knowledge of the world beyond the villages of their bush nation, which

The Reunion

stretch up and down hundreds of miles of rivers and streams. Others had visited Amerindian villages with their fathers and uncles during trading trips. And others wanted to become boatmen who worked the entire river for transporting food, materials, and people back and forth. They had heard stories from the boatmen about the areas where *bakrah* used big machines to move trees and dig up the earth, and they wanted to see that. But some youngsters worried because they had heard their parents say that the older boys were leaving them and the village to die while they sought work with *bakrah* miles away. They did not ever want to leave their families behind permanently. Most of the boys said that they simply wanted to grow up to be good hunters and good boatmen so that they could provide for their families. Some wanted to be medicine men or messengers, but they all said that this was not just their decision. Such a position must be decided by all the villagers.

An Africanism that has been with the bush people since their ancestors brought it across the Atlantic is the *anansi toree,* spider tales. These stories, told mainly to children and young teenagers, are always about Anansi, a clever and crafty spider who manages to outwit wrongdoers. The stories always carry a strong moral, which helps teach cultural values to the young. Special adults in the village, usually men, or older volunteers are charged with telling *anansi toree* to the young who delight in hearing them. Usually in the quiet of dusk or early evening children gather at a predesignated spot, generally the cottonwood tree or a special hut, and sit together on their *bangis* until the storyteller arrives to greet the group and make a few introductory remarks. In an evening's sitting, several stories are told, some evoking laughter, others causing distress or sadness, but each carrying some precept for the ethical development of the young people.

The following is a condensed version of one of the many *anansi* stories of the bush people. It was told to boys and girls of six to fourteen by a slender, cheerful gray-haired man.

There was once a man in a village far from here who was too lazy to plant and harvest his food. This man did not want to clear the fields and gather food for himself and his family. He only liked to sit at the tree and drink coconut milk and

The Reunion

Playing with first
frisbee.

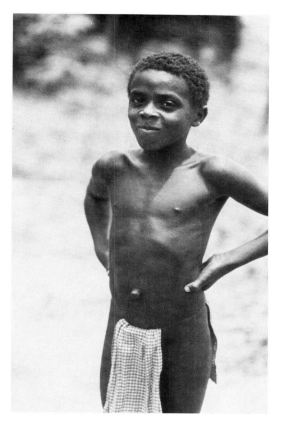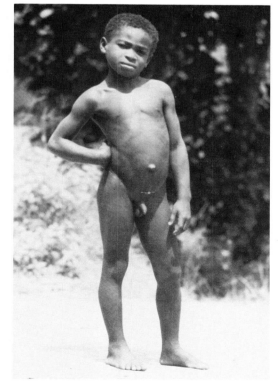

sleep while others worked and brought him food. But he did not have enough food to satisfy his large appetite. So late at night he would slip away from the village and go to the food storehouse in the forest and steal the food others had harvested. He would make the marks of the jaguar on the ground so the people would think that the large, dangerous cat had taken their food. He did this for many seasons.

One night when he was stealing food by the light of his bright torch, someone saw him. It was Anansi the spider, hanging from his web. When the man saw that Anansi was watching him, he became enraged and tried to kill Anansi with a stick. Anansi zigged and zagged many times to avoid his wild blows. Finally Anansi dropped to the ground and went into a hole. The man then pounded the earth around the hole until he was certain that he had crushed Anansi. Then he covered the hole with clay and a large stone so that even if Anansi had survived the crushing he could never leave the hole.

Many days later, the village headman, who was very worried about the frequent raids on the food supply, was studying the marks of the jaguar in order to determine his size and strength. He heard a bird above his head chirping one of the most beautiful songs he had ever heard. He looked up to see the bird, but something else caught his eye. It was a message that had been woven into a spider's web. While Anansi was zig-zagging to avoid the blows of the thief who was trying to kill him, he had spun out an important message in his web: "It is not the panther that steals your food. It is a man from your village who will think that I am dead from his hands." Anansi did not reveal the man's name.

The chieftain returned to the village and called all the people together in the center of the village and announced, "The panther that steals our food has two feet and he is among us. He was witnessed in this cowardly act by Anansi whom he tried to kill. But Anansi escaped and I have brought him home with me and tomorrow morning he will point the thief out to me." The people then left to return to their huts in great excitement and anticipation.

When the next morning came, all of the men and women assembled in the center of the village to see who would be named by Anansi as the culprit. But when the chieftain arrived there was no Anansi with him. The people were surprised. The chieftain asked if everyone in the village were present. They looked among themselves and found that one person was missing. That person was the lazy thief. They found that he had taken his boat and all other possessions and fled the village the night before, never to return. The chieftain turned to the villagers and said, "The guilty one hears footsteps and sees eyes that are not upon him and takes leave." Or, as we had learned during our childhood Sunday school lessons, "The guilty [wicked] flee when no man pursueth."

The Reunion

When boys and girls reach puberty, they no longer roam the village at will in the nude. Puberty rites vary in elaborateness from village to village and tribe to tribe. A girl, to signify that she has reached womanhood, can be washed at the river by a group of women in a secret, women-only ceremony, where flowers are placed on her head and tossed in her path as she walks out of the water and back into her hut. In the hut she is given a new loincloth, woven by her family and friends, and a colorful set of beads or shells to sling around her waist. The brownish color of the beads, which are partially obscured under the loin cloth, indicates that she has reached puberty. At marriage the color of her beads will be changed to yellow, and after her first child the color will change again, to red.

On several occasions we noticed that some of the women who had helped us in collecting plants and other tasks would without notice take leave from their huts and sometimes from the entire village for several days. When we inquired about their whereabouts we learned that they had gone off to the edge of the village to live in the women's *oso* (or menstrual hut). Apparently the practice is mandatory for all bush women. We also learned that rules governing the practice are made by the women themselves, and it is not viewed as negative. In fact, the women seem to enjoy this opportunity to get away from the village chores and family and join their friends in the woman's *oso* for several days of gossip and laughter.

Males of the bush culture are not circumcised. Like girls, when boys reach puberty at thirteen or earlier, they must wear loincloths. When they begin to grow pubic hair, they are given ceremonially blessed clothes by their parents and told never to appear nude in public again. Then they are considered men.

Premarital sex is seriously frowned upon in the bush nation, and almost every woman takes pride in maintaining her virginity until marriage at age sixteen or older. The men must respect the laws against promiscuity and generally begin to consider marriage at nineteen to twenty-five.

Teenage girls and boys are allowed to intermingle in certain group activities. They may dance together at some ceremonies, and a good dancer, male or female, is an asset to

The Reunion

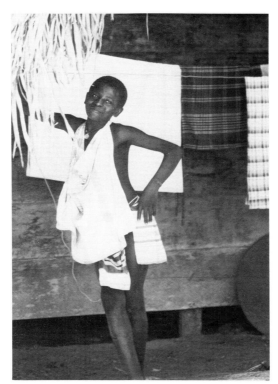

His first private hut—a
gift from his father.

A young brave.

the community. Girls and boys compete in swimming races, one of their favorite activities today as it was two hundred years ago. It is not unusual for the girl to win and be encouraged to do so by the other boys and girls. Stedman observed that

Swimming is their favorite diversion which they practice every day at least twice or thrice, promiscuously, in groups of boys and girls, like the Indians, when both sexes exhibit astonishing feats of courage, strength and activity. I have not only seen a negro girl beat a hardy [male] youth in swimming across the river Comewina but on landing challenge him to run a two mile race and beat him again, naked as they were; while all ideas of shame on the one side, and insult on the other, are totally unknown.

Boys and girls are tutored in the skills of survival and prosperous existence in the hostile rain forest from the time they can begin to master simple tasks. When they reach puberty, they are well prepared to perpetuate the life-styles, traditions, and culture of their ancestors.

The Ancestral Dance Ritual

One evening the village headman and several elders invited us to attend a special ritual ceremony held in honor of their ancestors. We were told that the head medicine man and the chief *liree* (teaching) man would get in touch with the spirits of the ancestors and teach the history of their people to all of the villagers. The eldest of the group said that this ceremony was sacred and that no outsider had ever been permitted to witness the spiritual rituals. He said that there had been a major meeting earlier by the ruling council to discuss whether we could be allowed to attend. Some, he said, had initially been against it, believing our presence could bring bad spirits. But the chieftain and other elders spoke in our behalf, saying, "These are brothers from another land. They too are African and are searching for the road back home. Our village is a station along that road, and we should honor them for their visit to our land." The visiting men were part of them, the elders said, and we have treated them as family because, having watched the visitors carefully, the elders found them "to be good in their hearts." The elder said that all of the others had finally agreed with the chieftain and decided to let us watch the sacred ritual. We were even allowed to bring our cameras and tape recorders to document the ceremony. We had to ask permission to photograph people and events, since the villagers sometimes violently resented the aiming of cameras (or anything else, for that matter) in their direction. With the chieftain's and ruling council's permission, we could photograph at will throughout the village with the assumption that it had been cleared with all of the villagers.

The ancestral ritual had begun. We could hear drums in the distance. They were being beaten at sites within the village and along the river. Faint drumbeats came from distant drummers in other villages, an ancient but effective communication system calling villagers from miles around. Lavishly decorated boats with painted and metal designs could be seen coming down the river. People from outlying villages arrived in large numbers, men and women wearing brightly colored togas and loincloths and children with patterned criss-cross sashes across their chests and long, colorful loincloths. The little girls' hair was arranged and styled with care, some with little puffs all over and others with braids.

The Reunion

The chieftain's
granddaughter.

A young boy acts
out dance of rebel
ancestors.

Telling *anansi* stories.

Village leader prepares
for the ancestral
veneration dance.

A medicine man
meditates before
dance.

Medicine man stands
to recite prayer.

Liree man prepares
to call dancers into
action.

Drummer sounds
the beginning of the
drama.

By the time we arrived at the end of the village near the river bank, the first part of the ceremony had begun. The elders, including the *liree* men, had begun to talk to the scores of villagers who had gathered around and were sitting on *bangis.* It is considered highly improper to sit on the ground, and almost everyone has a *bangi* carved by an uncle, son, nephew, friend, or himself. One *liree* man sat in front of the crowd accompanied by a special assistant, some of the elders, and a few chosen children who would become *liree* men themselves some day. As he spoke, his special assistant punctuated his remarks with an occasional "That is so," or "Yes, brother, that is the way it was."

Acting as official historian, the *liree* man was reciting the names of all of the headmen and, in some cases, the councils that had preceded the present *bossiah.* The audience sat quietly and reverently, and his chant recorded the years, the scores of years, the centuries. Our interpreter tried valiantly to keep pace in translating. We were astounded by the power of the *liree* man's memory. "And then there was Chief Abinta, a great man, he had a proud wife, Kaiaya, a strong woman who could paddle her boat for many miles and through the great, bad waters with no difficulty."

The bush dwellers showed serious inquisitive faces, both the young and old. The teenagers, too, were respectful of their elders, sitting quietly, totally absorbed in the recitation, their eyes fixed on the *liree* men. It was a glorious sight, this audience of about three hundred people, all magnificently dressed, proud and absorbed in the pageantry celebrating their great history. Stedman described the very ancestors now being remembered by the sacred ritual, back in 1796, when he wrote, "their strong features . . . their bright black eyes, and fine teeth we are forced to admire . . . generally strong and muscular near the trunk, and slender toward the extremities; they have mostly a remarkable fine chest, but are small about the hips. The buttocks are more prominent . . . the thighs are strong as also the arms above the elbows." The description holds thoroughly true for their descendants.

The introductory historical chant continued for about two hours, when the *liree* man ended his talk and asked the group to stand. He poured a libation of liquid from a gourd on the ground before him, reciting a verse of a short prayer

The Reunion

The drama begins.

Two dancers act out
ritual drama.

Medicine man performs
ritual.

each time he poured. Many of the older villagers joined in with refrains like *"Ee ba, quiti-quiti"* (never never), *"Gan Tanee Gan Gadu"* (thank you, Great God). At the end of the prayer, many embraced the *liree* man.

The excitement of the crowd grew more intense. Older and middle-aged men brought drums into the center of the village and set them in front of the crowd. Many of the women stood together to one side of the drums. In unison they chanted *Ouuuu,"* at a high pitch, the chants held for about a minute each. They seemed to be encouraging spiritual stimulation for the men pounding the drums in short intervals. In the center, between the drummers and the crowd, a mammoth fire was built with logs and boards men had brought in from the forest.

As the fire blazed larger, the drums beat louder and more frantically, and the people grew more excited. Many were chanting songs, some were dancing, and the children stood spellbound by the entrancing events. Occasionally a small infant, frightened by the unaccustomed noise and activity, would begin to cry. The smoke grew stronger, the wood on the fire turned to burning coal, and the crowd moved back to form a big circle.

Emerging from the smoke a few figures could be distinguished moving in and out of the smokelike phantoms. They were led by Apauti, who had a red cloth wound around his head and wore a white wrap. Their bodies were covered with the sacred white clay, *pemba dottee.* Some among them were medicine men, and they wore copious decorations around their necks, including African cowrie shells. Some of their neck decorations were purely cosmetic, others contained tribal medicines. They began a haunting, complex dance, a historical dance performed several times a year to remind them of their proud history. The dance is also a dramatic lesson to their young people of the way their forebears arrived in this land from their native African villages on slave ships, how they plotted cunning escapes, and fought a long guerrilla war to free themselves of their enslavers.

The men darted and pranced, demonstrating the plight of the slaves' life, the horrible working conditions, the brutal beatings. One man beat another, stage-punching, as the second fell helplessly to the ground. The drama showed the Europeans kicking and beating the fallen slaves. It continued

The Reunion

with a mime showing how the slaves began stealing away from the plantations by night and meeting their revolutionary brothers and sisters in the bush. If caught, the ritual dance demonstrated, they'd have one or more of their limbs chopped off by a European enslaver for such transgression.

The dancers and *liree* men continued their dance-drama, playing the roles of Africans fleeing to the bush immediately upon setting foot on shore, or following a time of recuperation from the inhuman conditions of their voyage on the slave ship. In the bush, the dancers demonstrated, all organized into groups of freedom fighters, vowing to "free all of our brothers and sisters from the *bakrah yorica.*" The dancers knelt in a small huddle to show how their ancestors plotted strategy. Then they crawled about on their bellies, preparing for the attack on a plantation, or an ambush of a squad of Dutch soldiers or mercenaries. Some of the men leapt into the air, shooting imaginary muskets at the enemy, and started crawling as they would through the bush, guerrilla style. As the dance intensified, the spirits of ancestral warriors were said to enter their bodies. Many in the audience went into trances, gyrating in imitation of the dancing medicine men.

The dancing medicine men, when they felt possessed by the Kromanti spirit, the warrior spirit, which is impervious to swords, bullets, fire, or any other weapon, continued the ritual in what appeared to be a trance. They leapt into the burning fire for so long they had to be pulled out by others, yet no one seemed even slightly burned or injured. Some men chopped at their bodies with sharp machete knives, seeming to connect with the knife each time. Yet the knives did not cut them and there was no bleeding. The women chanted the refrain even louder than earlier, "ouououououou . . ." One woman was so overcome with emotion and her feeling for the spirit of Kromanti that she headed for the fire, but other women grabbed her and tried to restrain her. It took many women to hold her down; she was throwing them off like feathers.

A man of about eighty became so possessed with the warrior spirit that he began to demonstrate his invincibility by jumping up and down on long sharp thorns from a large tree branch. The sharp thorns did not seem to damage his feet.

The Reunion

He went to the fire and reclined gracefully, in a slow, deliberate manner, in the flames and burning coals. A group of men rushed over and pulled him out of the smoke and flames. He was unscathed and carried on with his dance, still struggling to fight off the unseen enemies of the warrior spirit.

After more than two hours of this frenzied dance, Apauti and another medicine man began shouting in the Kromanti language, the sacred African language known only to the older men. They were taught it by their fathers, and they by their fathers and uncles, and so on back to the original African arrivals, a language primarily Ghanaian in origin. The two medicine men preached loudly and gestured to each other in the Kromanti language as if to say that "My *obeah* is even stronger than your *obeah.*" Finally they embraced each other, laughing and saying to each other, "We have really felt the spirit of the ancestors today." The women came out to embrace the men, squeezing them with one hand at the waist briefly, to say, "You have preached a great sermon today." The rituals were repeated, with intervals for rest.

When everyone was exhausted, the medicine men went through the smoke and departed for their huts. The drummers left, and the crowd dispersed. The sky filled with clouds minutes after the dance. The wind blew fiercely, whistling through the trees. The crowd scattered throughout the village as they ran for their huts. It was strange to us, so much like a Hollywood invention. But the people believed that the spirits had heard them and were answering them with strong rains, which they readily welcomed for their crops. The strong winds, thunder, and electrical storm were not so welcome but were accepted as "God's speaking in his mighty way." In our later visits to the deep bush country of Surinam, we witnessed other ritual dances; there were hard rainstorms within minutes of the end of every ritual.

The Reunion

The Birth of a Child

Mayaya, who has lived for eighteen harvest seasons, is about to have her first child. She has spent most of her days at her hut during the last month, weaving cloth and cleaning. Her husband, Quasiba, goes hunting each day, and her family and friends attend to her needs. She visits her women friends and spends much of the time talking about the baby. Her strenous work—tending the garden near the hut, preparing the cassava bread, and collecting pails of water for cooking—continues up to the time she feels the baby coming. Little girls of the village like to visit her to ask about the baby and see if her stomach has grown bigger. If they are lucky, some of the girls will be selected by the midwife to assist in delivering the baby, a practice enabling them to learn the techniques of midwifery for their own generation. Most important, Mayaya pays frequent visits to her *obeah* man, the medicine specialist who prescribes herbs and offers prayers. Most of these herbs and solutions are applied externally, very few are consumed orally, and all have been used for centuries by the women and, before them, by their ancestors in Africa.

In her small native village of Bōāsē (which means "I have got you in my hand"), Mayaya spent a morning conducting a spiritual cleansing ritual for her baby. Greatly rotund and tight, her stomach seemed to have reached its limit for expansion. She wore a simple loincloth wrapped around her hips and below her stomach. She stood in front of a large bowl that contained several herbs and the egg of a fowl, these elements of ritual perscribed by her *obeah* man. Straining slightly, Mayaya bent over the bowl from her waist, in a deep bow, and scooped some of the liquid solution out of the bowl, massaging her stomach with the liquid. She repeated the bowing and rubbing ritual again and again, now and then chanting a prayer. No one interfered with the ritual. People passed quietly and went about their work while Mayaya massaged and prayed. The ritual completed, a village elder gave us permission to speak with Mayaya about the ritual and to visit her in her spacious hut.

Our ripely pregnant hostess offered us *bangis* to sit on, said she was pleased that we wanted to visit her, and hoped that we had brought goodwill to her house. She pointed to

Pregnant woman
washes her stomach
with a solution blessed
by her *obeah* man.

Mother and son.

the magnificently carved *bangis* and proudly told us that her husband had made them for her. She gestured toward a tiny child's *bangi* and pointed to her stomach. Smiling, she said that her husband had carved this one for their child. If it is a girl, she said, he will put more decorations on it. If the baby is a boy, he will carve a special hunter's bow on the sides.

Did she want a boy or a girl? We asked. It is God's will that determines the sex of the baby, Mayaya told us, and she would be happy with God's decision; she only hoped the child would be strong and healthy. Later she confessed that she preferred a girl so that she could enjoy her companionship and teach her knowledge of plants, food, and other things that women know about. Her husband, she said, wanted a boy, a strong hunter who would help to provide food for the village.

We asked her why she rubbed her stomach with the egg and herbs from the bowl. She laughed shyly, said that this was women's talk, and said she was surprised at our interest. We explained that this practice was unheard of in our country, and we wanted to learn more about it so that we could teach others. "Don't the women of your land practice this ritual?" she asked. If not, what do they do when they are about to have a child?"

We then spent about an hour explaining through our interpreter the process of childbirth in the United States. She listened attentively as we described large specialized hospitals, so far from Mayaya's cultural experience and hard to comprehend, and medicines, midwifery, and the nature of the delivery.

At the end of our discussion she seemed spellbound and overjoyed. She said that we had given her so much knowledge that it made her feel even larger, and she wondered if we would be willing to repeat this interesting story to the other women in the village. We assured her that we would be happy to. She said that since we were so kind as to tell her a story about the women in our land, she would tell us about childbirth among her people.

She said that women become pregnant early after they had been "taken by a man," in other words, wed. From the first few months of pregnancy through childbirth, three times a day they perform traditional rituals taught to them by the *obeah* man or woman when he or she prescribes the herbal medicine. The ritual we had watched was called *waei wiri*. The raw egg was for continued fertility and represented a healthy birth, and the herbs soaked in river water would make her child strong and great. All of the contents of the bowl had been blessed by the *obeah* man. She said she was expecting the birth any day, because the fetus had told her by movement, and she knew that almost one full harvest season had passed since the time she had become pregnant. Afanti, a highly respected midwife, would deliver the baby in Mayaya's hut. Although she admitted to being a little frightened, she was also very excited about the idea of "creating someone of her own and someone who would help develop their village."

Eight days after we met Mayaya, Counter was out in the bush collecting herbal medicines with an old woman knowledgeable about therapeutic plants, and Evans was at a nearby creek watching a man and his son carve a canoe from a fallen tree. Children were sent on urgent errands to collect us and bring us to Mayaya's hut; she was about to give birth. Each of us ran back with the children to Mayaya's hut in the far corner of the village, somewhat surprised by the request, and wondering a little about why we had been summoned. We had not been forewarned that there would be such an invitation, nor had we spoken with Mayaya for more than a week. When we arrived, there were several women and a group of young girls gathered outside the hut. They had somber looks on their faces as they sat down and arranged themselves near the entrance of the hut.

Afanti came to the door and spoke to the small girls, asking four of them to join her inside. The midwife told us that Mayaya had asked that her new friends from far away be present when the baby was born. We were also told that her husband was off in the forest clearing a field for planting and was not expected soon. We were asked to take a seat outside the hut and wait, which we did, though we felt a little awkward.

We could see inside the hut, and Afanti was busily scurrying around a fire on which she was boiling water and cooking some strange-smelling herbs. She would take the pot containing the herbs, let Mayaya inhale some of the vapor

The Reunion

154

Mother and son.

Mother and daughter.

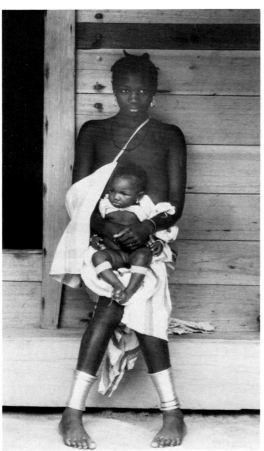

Counter entertains
child.

and smoke for a few seconds, then take it away. Then she'd take the warm water in a cloth and rub it over Mayaya's stomach. Afanti and the small girls finally helped Mayaya out of her hammock, walked with her behind a palm frond partition near the back of the hut, and told her to squat. We could hear Afanti directing the young girls and trying to sooth Mayaya. We could hear mild moans from Mayaya, and although we could no longer see her, we judged from her moans that she was about to deliver.

The outside group's attention turned to several small boys making a commotion as they ran from the bush toward the hut. Following them was Mayaya's husband, Quasiba, who had been fetched back to the village by the little messengers. He seemed nervous and happy. Older men walked up to greet him as he neared the hut, some of them with jugs and gourds of rum or palm wine. Quasiba took a gourd, poured some liquid onto the ground, and said a prayer. He drank the rest of the gourd's contents hurriedly. Several other men did likewise, and one of the elders beckoned us to join them. We were given gourds filled with strong palm wine. Each of us poured libations on the ground and said prayers for the health of the child and the happiness of the family. Our interpreter translated, and the people showed their pleasure with smiles and hand clasps.

Afanti emerged from the hut and paused. Everyone stared at her anxiously. She broke into a broad smile and said that it was a boy and was very healthy. By this time a large group of women had gathered outside the hut, and they began singing in unison. The young girls who had assisted Afanti came outside to join in the singing, and were embraced and congratulated. It was a joyous and cheerful song that was sung for the mother so that she would pass through her pain cheerfully. It also contained a prayer for the child's health and well-being. The father was excited but restrained as the older men congratulated him. He walked over to the door of his wife's hut but stayed outside because men are not allowed to enter a woman's hut during childbirth under normal circumstances.

The strong cries of the infant were heard, and Afanti appeared in the doorway with the naked child, who kicked his legs and stretched out his arms vigorously as he cried. The

The Reunion

women all cheered because such lively movement is a sign of good health. And they commented on the beauty of the child. Afanti handed the boy to his emotionally overwrought father. Quasiba took the child cautiously, held him near his chest briefly, and timidly gave him back to Afanti. Suddenly he was ecstatic. We too were given the baby; Afanti said that Mayaya wanted us to hold him. The father nodded his approval; we held the newborn and said, "moi, moi" (beautiful, beautiful). We could feel his strong stomach muscles as he cried. Taking the baby back into the hut, Afanti asked everyone to leave Mayaya and the baby in peace, and she disappeared into the hut. The gathering broke up, and the father was escorted to a nearby hut belonging to one of the older men with whom he had been drinking, no doubt to continue their celebration.

Meanwhile Afanti told us about the delivery. She said that the mother drinks only fresh water blessed with certain leaves when the baby is about to be delivered. The mother squats, young girls helping to steady her balance, while the midwife helps her to force the baby downward. The midwife and one small girl assistant are the only ones who touch the baby as they secure it during its emergence. Before touching the baby, they hold their hands over the hot steam from the boiling water to keep them clean. According to Afanti, most midwives observe this practice because the infant seems to stay healthier, and the baby's body, which is warmer than the midwife's hands, is not shocked by cool hands. The umbilical cord is cut swiftly with a sharp stone or knife which is held over the hot steam for several minutes by one of the young apprentices. The umbilical cord and placenta are immediately buried behind the mother's hut in a brief ceremony, which includes prayers for the infant's health, prosperity, and the hope that he will never stray far from his mother's home or lose concern for her well-being.

Our talk with Afanti over, she departed for her hut and we walked down the river to bathe. To our amazement we saw Mayaya and her hour-old baby wading in the river as she bathed the child and chanted prayers. Several small girls and young women stood around her chanting lovely melodies. When Mayaya left the water, walking through a crowd of little girls who were now giving her flowers, homemade soap,

The Reunion

and other gifts, she returned to her hut. She wrapped her baby in a thick cloth and secured him to her back with a second cloth. Only about two hours after the delivery of her child, Mayaya began working around her hut, pulling up small trees and weeds and digging up the cassava plants. Such hardiness is commonplace. Stedman was impressed with the strength and activity of women delivering babies in the 1770s. He wrote of the black women, "They bring their offspring into the world without pain, and like the Indian women resume their domestic employment even the same day."

The Reunion

**Nutrition,
Health, and
Medicine**

The bush people get most of their food by hunting for wild game, fishing, and planting. They appear to have a well-balanced diet, and no malnutrition or poverty is evident. Methods of hunting and gathering, within the strict limitations of the rain forest environment, require considerable knowledge and skill.

Many would call their food-gathering techniques primitive by modern standards, but one of our experiences led us to conclude that the bush people have a refined knowledge of the food chain of the rain forest. We refer to a *neku* fishing session, where the young people of an entire village were taught the art and science of chemical fishing. The villagers, led by Apauti, collected large amounts of the roots and vines of a plant called *neku* from deep in the jungle. The vinelike plant was transported to an area known to be replete with fish of all sizes. Adults strew the *neku* plants over logs or stones and pounded them to a pulp, using large wooden sticks and stones. The children imitated the adults, pounding the *neku,* so that they soon all waded into the stream with the well-beaten plants. Disregarding the dangers of the stream—the poisonous snakes, piranha, and electric eels— they pushed the plants back and forth in the water. The plants released a milky substance that clouded the stream white and floated slowly dowstream.

In the wake of the *neku* substance, we could see small fishes floating to the surface of the river, still struggling. Soon large fish were affected as well, and the villagers filled their baskets with fish. An electric eel, about four feet long and five inches in diameter, struggled in the milky water, it too apparently affected by the chemical. Apauti speared it and pulled it out of the water. He severed its spinal cord at a couple of places along its back, explaining to the children how it was done but not allowing them to touch the eel. Cutting the spinal cord prevented further movement in the animal and affected its ability to produce the more than 100 volts of electricity of which it is capable. Such a shock could kill anyone.

Playfully we feigned ignorance of the electric eel and went toward it as if to touch it. The children grabbed our hands and legs to restrain us, and the adults tried to warn us against touching or lifting the eel. Without our translator,

160

Boys pound *neku* for
milky extract.

Some small fish and a
large eel caught a few
minutes after *neku* was
put in water.

neither the children nor the adults could explain to us in words that we would be shocked if touched the eel, so they all raised arms to their chests and held their fists clenched while they made the staccato-like sound, "*dit, dit dit, dit, dit, dit.*"

Enough fish had been collected, so the fishing party divided the catch, including the eel, and headed home. That evening most of the village enjoyed what was to us an old-fashioned fish fry.

The bush dwellers' *neku* plant is *Tephrosia toxicaria* (sinapou), a rotenone that can block a fish's ability to take in oxygen through the gills. We'd suspected it might be a nerve toxin of some sort and wondered why it had no harmful effect on the people who consumed the fish poisoned by it. But it is a chemical, native to both Africa and South America, which has no deleterious effects on humans, simply stunning fish by temporarily blocking their breathing apparatus.

Fishing is also done by string and hook, bow and harpoon arrow. Traditional nets and traps, similar to the ones they have used for centuries, are also used. The fish consumed by the bush people range in size from four inches long to large basslike fish and piranha. We had always thought of piranha as small fish about three to five inches long, but the ones we encountered in the Surinam and French Guiana bush were often over twelve inches long and exhibited remarkably large, razor-sharp teeth. These piranha, which represent a very important protein source in the bush diet, are caught with relative ease.

One day we witnessed a most unusual fishing technique involving a hook and string. A man of about sixteen was cutting small pieces of meat that had been soaked in a gourd of animal blood and put them on a large, strong metal hook. The hook was cast into the river stream on the long string, and the attached meat sank quickly beneath the surface. Within a few minutes there was usually a bite, evidenced by agitation in the water. The fish hooked, the young man yanked the line out of the water, over his head, and onto the bank near him. The catch: a foot-long piranha, still snapping wildly and flopping around. The fisherman did not touch the fish—one snap of the teeth could have removed one of his fingers. He took a large stick, pounded the fish until it no

The Reunion

Fish caught with bow
and arrow.

Piranha caught with hook.

Piranha heads, ready to cook.

longer moved, then took a long machete and chopped off the head. Only then did he attempt to remove his valuable hook from the piranha's mouth.

Men and young boys fish in this manner for piranha, but some of the older men (and neighboring Indians) harpoon piranha with bow and arrow. For this technique, they toss some leftover innards of a *pingo* (small wild pig) or other animal into a slowly flowing stream. Within minutes, piranha appear near the surface, tearing at the innards. The hunters shoot their arrows into the swelling commotion near the fish and almost invariably pull out a piranha by the string attached to the arrow. They pound and decapitate the fish and cook them.

Piranha and other fish are generally smoked and preserved, or boiled in a pot, and eaten with rice or cassava bread. We roasted piranha over a small fire and fried some in the vegetable oil we had brought with us. They were delicious no matter how they were prepared. They have a sweet, gamey taste, like some ocean fish.

All tribes of the bush nation use fish traps. They are long cone-shaped baskets, sprung when a large fish enters and seizes the bait, which forces the bent stick connected to the door to swing to its erect position. Nets, woven by the men are used for night fishing. A bright torch held over the water by night attracts schools of fish that are easily caught in fine but sturdy string nets.

For meat, the bush people hunt the wild pig or *pingo,* the agouti (a large rodent, which they call *kuni kuni*), the tapir or bush cow, and, rarely, the anteater. They eat a small tender species of monkey, a basic part of the neighboring Indians' diet, either roasted over a fire or boiled. These African-descended people also eat a large green iguana and a small bush deer.

The hunt for tapir can take days of careful tracking in the deep bush. The hunter is cautious because the dreaded jaguar also hunts the tapir and is often close by when one is spotted. Locating the tapir is the challenge, for once it is tracked down, the bush dwellers are confident of killing it by a single shotgun blast or arrow. The natives tie the fallen animal's feet together and hang their prize from a stick, which two men carry on their shoulders. Back in the village,

The Reunion

Small wild pig.

Hunter catches small
bird.

Hunter displays a
monkey he shot for the
day's meal.

they skin it and divide the meat up into sections, sharing it with their families and with anyone else in the village who needs it.

Wild pigs are hunted with shotguns. *Pingo* travel in herds of ten to twenty and follow one bull leader blindly, even to their death. Some of these wild pigs weigh over two hundred pounds and possess long and deadly curled tusks. In one hunting ground our native friends located a herd of about fifteen wild pigs. We closed in on them, and they panicked and started to run wildly in all different directions, the lead male running a ferocious charge toward our group. We inexperienced non–bush dwellers had our hunting initiation: With a seventy-pound bow Counter took aim at one of the full-tusk males as it charged, but the arrow hit the *pingo* in the center of the head and bounced off the animal as it continued to charge. Evans, standing as backup with a borrowed shotgun, let off a quick shot, which found its mark and dropped the animal several feet from Counter.

There would be no posing for pictures with this prize: the rest of the herd continued to charge. The bush men yelled "jump into the trees" and began leaping into the lower branches of the nearest tree. Mere seconds later, the charging animals passed under our feet. As the last one passed, the bush men leapt from the trees and started firing into the rear flanks of the *pingo*. Three more fell. We were happy to have brought down four, more than enough for a village feast. Back in the village that night, the four animals were skinned, prepared by the women, and roasted over a fire. Some of the meat was preserved by smoking it. The happy feast lasted for several hours, the villagers feted with stories of the hunt and great hunters of the past.

Ask bush dwellers what fowl they consider delectable, and they name the (large beak) toucan bird and several smaller species of songbirds. Adventurous bands of young boys with slingshots hunt *sutti mofu* or small birds that they roast and eat on the spot. If they catch many, they bring them back to the village to share with brothers and sisters who delight in the tender meat of the small birds. Almost every village keeps domestic chickens for laying eggs, and occasionally for food.

The green plantain, bananas, yams, corn, and cayenne pepper are important in the diet. Other than plantains, the

The Reunion

bush people eat few vegetables. Their lack of interest in cultivating and eating vegetables is exemplified in this typical statement: "Vegetables are caterpillar food, not for human consumption."

Fruits enjoyed by bush dwellers include wild limes, pineapples, watermelons, lemons, and oranges. They have peanuts, called *pinders,* red and green peppers, and okra. Both pigeon (or Angola) peas and maize are grown in abundance in fields far from the villages. Pigeon peas grow on a plant about eight to ten feet high. There are five to six peas in a single pod, which are flat like lentils and reddish brown in color. Stedman described the Surinam blacks of the eighteenth century as being extremely fond of them.

Rice, or *alesi* as the natives call it, has been a primary carbohydrate staple of the Surinam bush people since their ancestors arrived as slaves on the Continent. This rice is not grown in water but is a dry rice grown in cleared jungle fields miles from the villages. There are small camps of several huts built around the fields, used to house men who cleared the fields or women who harvested the rice when they did not want to travel the long journey back to the main village at night. Some huts serve as storage bins for the harvested rice.

Stedman described the Surinam rice as having "height of 4 feet, with furrowed stalks, and in appearance not unlike wheat. . . . The leaves are like those of reeds: the seeds are produced somewhat like barley and grow on each side of the spikes or ears alternately. The grains are oval, and if good, white, hard and transparent." This eighteenth-century picture describes precisely the rice that we found in current use in the bush villages.

When the women harvest the rice, they arrange it in small bundles or sheaves as in biblical days. They pile these bundles into large baskets and carry them back to the village, usually on their heads. It is a beautiful procession, a single line of harvesters moving gracefully along a jungle path with large baskets of rice on their heads.

Once the rice is brought into the village, the women place the bundles in great, heavy, wooden mortars called *mata*. These thirty to sixty-pound (sometimes painted) wooden devices have a twelve-inch-deep bowl about fifty inches in circumference and are cut from a single tree. The women use

The Reunion

Women harvest rice.

Women carry rice from
fields to village.

ten to twenty-five-pound wooden pestles to pound the rice (and other grains) until the hull is removed. More magnificent than the harvest scene is that of a group of ten to thirty women, three to a mortar, heartily pounding the grain in unison as they sing.

The pounding noise made by the powerful women seems to shake the earth as the three pestles strike the mortar within seconds of each other in a precise rhythm. The rhythm of this beat sets the children standing nearby to dancing. Even with this heavy pounding, it seems that not a grain is spilled on the ground. The hull removed from the grain, the women are ready to push the grain from the mortar by hand onto a broad, carved, painted wooden plate. The lighter hull is shaken up into the air, leaving the heavier, valuable grain behind. The same procedure is carried on today throughout West Africa and has been passed down over ten generations in the Surinam bush. Stedman said in the 1700s that certain foods "are put into wooden mortars and beaten by candle-light with heavy wooden pestles, like rice in Gado-Saby. . . . At this exercise the Negroes wonderfully keep time and always sing a chorous."

The rice fields lie from about five to twenty miles from the village and are literally hidden beyond a labyrinthine array of paths and fallen-tree bridges. We were at the point of exhaustion before we reached a distant rice field, but the natives seemed to cover long distances without perspiring. We asked the people to explain why they planted their rice fields (and sometimes yam, peanut, and cassava fields) so far away from their home village, knowing that this practice dated at least from the eighteenth-century when Stedman described it, but wanting to find out whether the same rationale still existed in the minds of the people.

When we first asked the question of a small group of villagers who were traveling with us to the rice fields, they answered simply, "We do not know. That is the way it has always been."

We asked, "Why has it always been this way?"

They answered again, "We do not know, it is just this way."

But because in this case we felt that we were among people who would not be offended by our persistent queries, we asked again. "But why? Surely your parents must have told

The Reunion

Pounding and
winnowing dry rice.

Pestle hits mortar with
rice.

Pounding oil nuts.

Tending private
cassava garden.

you why you hide your food grounds so many miles or even days by foot away from your home village."

The young people said they honestly did not know why; they only knew that it was their tradition. But with an exasperated sigh, one of the older men in the group said, "Look, it is this way for as long as my people have been in the bush; we have had to hide our food grounds and much of our harvest far from our villages so that if unforeseen dangers arise in the village and we have to flee, our food will be protected."

"What," we said, "do you mean by unforeseen dangers?"

"Well," he said, even more annoyed, "any dangers, like outsiders coming in to attack our village and capture us for *bakrah schlaffa* (white man slaves)."

The answer was over three hundred years old. Just as their freedom-fighting ancestors did in the seventeenth and eighteenth centuries to protect their food supply from the colonial armies thrown against them, these twentieth-century bush dwellers also hide and camouflage their crops in case similar groups attack them today. In the days of their rebellious ancestors, the soldiers burned their crops and fields to starve them out. The rebels knew that it takes only weeks to rebuild villages but months to regrow food. Thus the philosophy of defending their food supply exists just as do the traditional techniques of planting and harvesting it.

The Bush Afro-Americans make a butter by melting the fat of palm tree worms, and another butter is made from peanuts. A major source of cooking fat or oil comes from the large brown *mareepa* nut of the palm plant. They pound *mareepa* nuts with a heavy metal or pestle to remove the hull, then crush the contents down for its fat. The oil is stored in bottles and calabash gourds until it is ready for use.

The most widely used carbohydrate source in the bush is the bitter, or manioc cassava. This large potatolike plant is the root of a leafy green stalk that grows several feet high. This plant is molded into cakes of bread by both the bush people and the Indians. But it has to be thoroughly cleaned and processed before it is made into bread because of the deadly poisons it contains. Once it is harvested, the women wash the cassava in river water to remove any parasites or insects. The hull is peeled from the root, leaving a large

The Reunion

white pulp, which is rubbed over a serrated board until it is reduced to a mushlike wet meal.

The mushy substance is stuffed into an intricately woven tube-shaped basket called a *matapí,* which is about six feet long and nine inches in diameter. The loop on the upper end of the tube basket is secured to a pole extending from the roof of the hut. A long pole is slid through the loop on the bottom of the tube basket, and one end of the pole is put under a large immovable object while the woman presses her weight against the other end, causing the straw basket to elongate and squeeze inward. This process drains off the juices containing the poisonous substance. The juices can be used as an insecticide, a rodent killer, or, in rare instances, a suicide potion. When most of the juice has been drained from the meal, it is shaken out of the *matapi* and allowed to dry. Dried, it looks like cornmeal.

It is sifted, mixed with water, and poured onto circular, metal hot plates where it is baked into a thin, round, hard, bread cake, three feet or more in diameter. Once it hardens on one side, it is flipped over to the other. When it is thoroughly cooked, it is placed either on the roof of the house for storage or in a dry place in a food storage hut.

This bread is a daily staple of the bush dwellers. Even when traveling long distances by canoe, they always have large pieces of cassava bread with them as their main food source. When they are hungry, they dip a piece of bread in the river to soften it and eat it as they move along. Cassava bread is similar to the hoe cakes of cornbread made in the South from cornmeal. We became so accustomed to it that we could not distinguish it from the corn bread we had eaten back home.

In most villages sugar cane is cultivated in small family plots or large village plots. The candy of the jungle, it satisfies the sweet tooth and can be made into pleasant, stimulating soft drinks (or rum). We ate cane almost every day as a desert, after our evening meal, but the villagers do not eat it regularly, and perhaps their rewards for such abstinence are their good, white teeth.

After each meal, children and adults break a small twig from an orange tree or some other fragrant tree and chew it thoroughly. Such practices serve both for brushing teeth and

The Reunion

Preparing cassava
meal by grating.

Sifting the dry,
processed cassava
meal.

Grated cassava meal is
put into straw basket.

The poisonous liquid
is strained from the
cassava.

Cassava cakes drying
in sun.

Cooking cereal.

Barking coconut with machete.

Mentally retarded boy
using red plant extract
to remove parasites
from dog.

Pounding the rice
harvest.

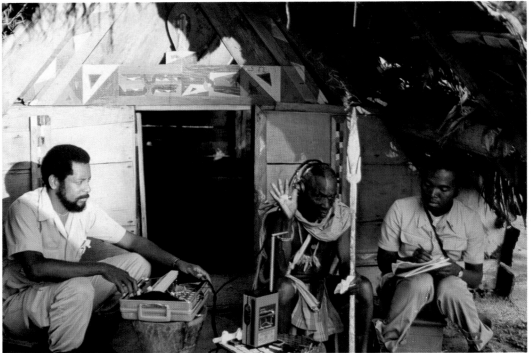

Special medical test
on girl suspected of
hearing problem.

Medical test on old
medicine man.

for general oral hygiene. Stedman wrote of the Surinam Africans in the 1700s, "His teeth are constantly kept as white as ivory; for this purpose he uses nothing but a sprig of orange-tree, bitten at one end, until the fibres resemble a small brush; and no negro, male or female, is seen without this little instrument, which has besides the virtue of sweetening the breath."

Their well-balanced diet helps make the Bush Afro-Americans a strong and healthy people with a probable average life span of about fifty-six years. Their diet comprises a variety of readily available meat protein, starch, and a few leafy green plants.

Health problems peculiar to the bush tribes include a predominance of eye cataracts, particularly in old age. The medicine man treats some cases, but his help seems virtually ineffective and the condition often ends in blindness. The cause of widespread cataracts is unknown but could be related to genetic, parasitic, or dietary factors.

In one tribal group we found high-frequency (nerve-involved) hearing impairment. Handicaps in any society, sensory deficits can spell tragedy in bush societies where livelihood can depend on hunting skills. One bush villager complained that he could not hear footsteps of animals when he hunted. Having lost the ability to gather food, he had to depend on the younger men for much of his livelihood. He knew of no possible cause of his hearing difficulty but said that some other older villagers seemed unaffected by this malady.

We conducted audiological tests on him and others who complained of hearing losses and finally screened the whole village for auditory problems. In some people we found fairly commonplace hearing losses due to ear infections and blockage, but in a high percentage of the middle-aged and elderly, there was evidence of high-frequency hearing loss.

This kind of hearing impairment is usually found where people have been exposed to noisy environments or have congenital infections. Yet there is no excessive noise in the bush dweller's rain forest habitat, and they show no evidence of congenital infections. In a tribal group many miles away we found no evidence of widespread high-frequency hearing loss. The one obvious difference between the two villages was that one uses the manioc cassava as its main

The Reunion

carbohydrate staple and the other uses rice. The cassava plant contains chemicals that if not properly processed can cause serious neurological damage, particularly in the auditory nerve. We couldn't definitely attribute the hearing problems to inadequate processing of the cassava root, but we believe it might be a related factor.

American companies had donated hearing aids for use among the bush dwellers. When we put hearing aids on people who had been partially deaf for years, village sounds and voices and babies crying brought bright smiles to their faces. One woman cried at hearing her grandchild's voice for the first time and went out the next day and caught us a great supply of fish.

Mein Piki Dada, a village elder and former headman about seventy-five years old, was fitted with a hearing aid in his impaired ear. He beamed with delight at his renewed ability to hear, went around the village chattering to everyone, and ended up at the main meeting house of the village where he announced to other elders that now that his hearing had been restored, he wanted to be made village headman again. The position had been taken from him by younger men because he could not hear, he told them emphatically. They conceded that he had a lot of spirit for an old man, but they would not fulfill his request. From time to time we would see the vigorous Mein Piki Dada traveling through the rapids in a small canoe with great precision and speed. His paddling was majestic. No vigorous hard strokes at all—his paddles just touched the water lightly, as if he wanted to pat it gently in special spots.

Mein Piki Dada, pleased with his new hearing aid, even though it did not restore him as village headman, gave us his own hand-carved *obeah* staff. He had used it for more than sixty years; it had been his father's.

Serious illness among some of the elderly and children was treated by the medicine man. When the medicine man's treatment cannot help and the patient deteriorates beyond hope, the bush people may travel long distances downstream to the jungle clinics of missionary doctors from the Dutch Moravian Brothers Church.

The mother of a very sick infant refused to consider the four-day canoe ride downriver to the Moravian clinic, saying

Mein Piki Dada, in his
late seventies, is fitted
with a hearing aid.

Special medical test to
examine condition of
ears.

she "would not go to the missionary clinic because the doctors made you take their God before they give you medicine." Later when we met a Dutch missionary doctor in the clinic, he dismissed her accusation as nonsense. Communication must have broken down between the bush people and the missionaries because at least some of the bush people fear that the missionaries insist on conversion before treatment.

Most of the bush people have never seen a Western doctor. The Surinam Ministry of Health said that there were simply "not enough doctors in Surinam to service the interior of the country." Most doctors did not want to venture into the "wild and savage jungle."

Hypertension, a major health problem among U.S. Afro-Americans, is usually attributed to dietary factors. But some scientists have suspected that stress may also play an important role, that is, the stress of survival in an oppressive society. Here were Afro-Americans genetically similar to those in the United States but not subjected to the same stresses.

We invited a physician, Levi Watkins, Jr., to join us on a later trip to the bush to offer medical services to the people and to help gather data on the health of the bush people, to be turned over to the Surinam government. Dr. Watkins, a professor of cardiology at Johns Hopkins Medical School, spent two weeks with us in the rain forest, covered over one hundred miles by canoe, and saw upward of two hundred and fifty patients. He took off his shirt and treated everyone who came to the makeshift clinics we set up in the villages. He visited invalids in their huts and was rewarded with fruits, vegetables, and wood carvings from the people of the village.

From routine blood pressure measurements on the patients he treated and from the volunteer subjects in the villages, we found that the incidence of high blood pressure among the Bush Afro-Americans was significantly lower than that of blacks in the United States.

There was no evidence of sickle cell disease among the bush people, but some of the bush people carry the malaria parasite in their blood stream with no apparent ill effects. This might suggest that the sickling capacity was present and active in their bloodstreams, since it is believed that the purpose of the sickling is to destroy parasites in the blood.

The Reunion

Stedman wrote that during the period of slavery and the revolts, diseases like leprosy, yaws, and worm infections were often seen in the African-descended people. These problems were probably related more to the unhealthy conditions of slavery than to the people's general health. Leprosy is rarely seen in the jungle today but occurs in the modern capital city of Paramaribo. Also elephantiasis is much more prevalent in Paramaribo than in the bush.

In bush villages children rarely suffer mental retardation or physical defects. The two Down's syndrome victims we saw in separate villages seemed well integrated into village life and protected by their society, but they were not allowed to have children and, when they died, were given a unique burial. The bush people call them "God's special children."

A physical aberration seen regularly among the bush dwellers is the umbilical hernia. The natives consider the extremely long navel, the result of improper severance of the umbilical cord at birth, a hazard.

There are thousands of species of plants in the general Amazon area, and over the centuries the bush people, with help from the aboriginal Indians of the region, have screened many of them for use as medicines. Some of their medicines are known to outsiders and some are not. Possibly certain plants found in Surinam and the entire area of the Guianas were brought from Africa by slaves or slavers. The properties of some of the local plants were learned from the indigenous American Indians who seem to be masters of plant chemistry.

Few Americans know that much of their early pharmocopoeia was based on slave plant medicines. Two discoveries that laid the foundation for modern Western medicine were taken from African and South American knowledge of plants: African Calabar bean called eserine, and the South American Indians' resinlike curare plant substance.

In the 1800s, invading European enslavers were astounded by Nigerian tribes who engaged in a trial-by-ordeal ceremony called *esere.* The Europeans observed that if a tribesperson was accused of serious crime, such as severe harm to another person or selling captured tribal enemies as slaves to whites, he was subjected to an ordeal trial (*esere*) to determine guilt or innocence. If the person was guilty, he or she would die; if innocent he or she lived. The Europeans

Teaching young boys
plant medicine.

could not understand how the practice worked, and the Africans would not share the secret of this ritual with them. Later it was learned that at the heart of this ritual is a bean called *esere.* It contains a chemical called eserine (Physostigmine), which causes an abnormally exaggerated chemical activity between nerves and muscles. In the presence of this chemical the human nerves and muscles go into prolonged and uncontrollable activity, causing severe convulsions and eventual death.

This bean is given to the accused by the medicine man during an elaborate ceremony. The accused is asked to eat the ordeal fruit in the presence of the entire village while drums play to a crescendo. If the accused is guilty, he or she, having an implicit faith in the power of the medicine man, will eat the fruit very slowly and with great fear. Unbeknown to the accused, the very slow consumption of this plant will give it time to have its chemicals diffuse across the gut, enter the body proper and cause generalized convulsions, paralysis of the diaphragm, asphyxiation, and quick death. If the accused is innocent, he or she will have an unquestioning faith in the judicial powers of the medicine man and a confidence of their own innocence. The innocent will swallow the entire bean very quickly and defiantly and proudly walk around the crowd to proclaim his or her innocence. The rapid buildup of the chemical in the stomach will invariably cause massive vomiting so that all of the poison is ejected out of the stomach. The vomiting act itself is seen by the bush dwellers as purging the person of any evil within him, and he exonerates himself of the crime.

When the Europeans saw this medicine work, they confiscated some of it and took it to England, where medical scientist investigated it. It was found to have a profound accelerating effect on the heart and strength in activating paralyzed muscle. It became the foundation of modern physiology, but Africans are rarely given credit for the discovery of this medicine. What confounds scientists nonetheless is the question of just how the Nigerian medicine men screened this medicine from over 800,000 different species of plants in Africa and found its specific actions. Even in modern times and with modern technological screening techniques, this plant medicine has been located in only one other place on earth, Russia, in 1953. The Africans used this

The Reunion

chemical almost exclusively in sacred rituals and as a medicine. Europeans and Euro-Americans too use this plant today to treat certain nerve-muscle diseases; for war use it is called nerve gas.

The Bush Afro-Americans have a secret ritual that seems to resemble this African version in many details, but we were not able to watch it. For several years we searched for this plant medicine, or evidence of its usage by the *obeah* man, but have found only few people willing to discuss it. We believe that it is practiced in the sacred village of Dahomey. One medicine man who had observed a similar practice among the older priests of Dahomey described it in remarkable detail for us; however, we are still searching for proof.

The primary repository of village plant medicine, the *obeah* or medicine man, studies and researches plant medicine in a manner not totally unlike some scientific methods of modern societies. In the dense rain forest, an *obeah* man collects such plants as *singafu,* used to cure stomach ailments, which indeed contains chemicals beneficial to the treatment of minor stomach problems.

Apauti eventually let us observe his medical practice and several patients. Apauti and the medicine men are holistic and as such see medicine and religion as one. Their medical treatments of patients consist mainly of administering herbs and various potions made from those herbs, which they select from their stockpile of dried or freshly picked plants. While administering drugs, most often topically and sometimes internally by ingestion, they invariably chant a prayer or sing a spiritual song. The chant is as important to the healing process as the medicine, giving comfort to the sick patient and taking his or her mind off the malady. Often the medicine man dances or makes circular movement around the patient, and this too communicates the power of the medicine man and his familiarity with the healing spirits with which he is in contact.

One day, Counter complained of a severe and constant pain in his elbow. The problem had been diagnosed earlier at Harvard as an infected tendon. But it had since grown so severe as to make it hard to paddle a boat and pull a seventy-pound bow to the full position. Noticing the ailment,

Counter joins medicine
man in collecting
plants.

Medicine man treats
Counter's inflamed
elbow.

Apauti offered to treat the arm with his medicines. We had little faith in Apauti's healing abilities, since we were not immersed in his spiritual world, and our scientific background made us somewhat suspicious and less trusting of certain folk medical practices. But we had heard about effective treatments for people who suffered broken limbs from canoe accidents in the rivers, where broken limbs were said to have healed miraculously after treatment with bone softeners. We decided to try.

Apauti asked that the patient put on the loincloth given him when he first arrived in Pokaytee. This done, the medicine man took the arm and studied it, pushing it up and down, pressing in spots until he had localized the sensitive spots by Counter's reaction. He mixed a potion of river water and tiny leaves in a calabash gourd, stirred it briskly, and poured it over the kneeling patient's head, chanting prayers. He took a second gourd and mixed several herbs and river water in it. Taking one of the large, soaked herbs from the gourd, Apauti squeezed its juices onto the inflamed area of the elbow several times, rubbing the chemical into the elbow and chanting a prayer. The procedure went on about fifteen minutes.

Apauti finally put the herbs aside and picked up the two primary tools of all Bush Afro-American medicine men, the *fete* and the *saka*. (The *fete* is a hand-held wooden stick with long bird feathers and cowrie shells, which is said to have certain compartments that house secret chemicals. The *saka* is a round instrument made from dried gourds containing small pebbles and sand that cause a rattle when shaken. They are like the musical maracas.) The medicine man moved clockwise in a circle around the kneeling patient, chanting and occasionally tapping the sore elbow with the *fete*. At intervals, he interrupted this rite to apply small amounts of juice from hand-held herbs.

The ceremony ended, Apauti said, "You may get up and move your arms. The spirits have taken away your pain." Counter stood up. He no longer felt any pain in the arm, no matter how he moved it. He picked up his bow and for the first time in a few weeks could pull and hold it in the full position. We found it hard to believe that his arm had been cured by this unscientific process, but we had to admit that the pain was gone.

The Reunion

The Bush Afro-Americans sometimes use a poison called curare on the tips of their arrows in hunting land animals. This powerful chemical paralyzes the game after the arrow has struck its mark by blocking the chemical interaction between nerves and muscles. Its use was taught to the Bush Afro-Americans by the aboriginal Indians who discovered it among the 80,000 species of plants in Amazonia thousands of years before the Africans or Europeans set foot in South America. Here again, the ability of these and other so-called primitive people to screen and isolate for medicinal use a plant such as curare from such a large number has baffled modern scientists. Curare is used for medicinal treatment in the United States today and was also taken by early European explorers from the Indians of South America.

In a bush village everyone, even the children, know something about which plants are beneficial, which are not, which are to serve as medicine, and which are poisonous. Plants are the bush people's only source of medicine, and a knowledge of plants is crucial for survival. Women are the authorities on medicines for females and the varieties of plants that yield them. In attempts to gather information about female plant medicines from the women, we were met with shy laughter and told that this is woman's business, and men should have little interest in such things. One of the best ways to obtain information about women's plants was simply to spend time in the relaxing hours of the early evening sitting around with a group of women and talking. We sat in on women's hair-braiding sessions and had our hair braided while we chatted about plant medicines. The women were amused and would braid our hair in attractive African styles, laughing and talking all the while.

The conversations went like this. We'd say, "Today we saw a woman who could barely walk using a special plant medicine on her leg and hip. Will you tell me the name of that plant and where in the bush I can locate it?"

The women would giggle and reply, "Why do you want to know this? It is a woman's concern, not for men."

We would answer, "Yes that is true, but like your *obeah* man we like to study these plants to understand how they work."

The bush women would answer, "Only Gan Gadu and the spirits know how they work, and this secret has been locked

The Reunion

in the plant. We only know that they work for us because of the special things put in them by the spirits that make all things. Don't the women of your land know these plants? All women know these things."

We'd answer, "No. Our women can collect medicine which has been taken from plants by going to a special place to *mata* [barter] or to their *obeah* man or woman, who will give them medicine."

The reply would come, "Well, if your women do not know the plants, how do they have children?"

We'd answer, "With the help of their medicine man or medicine woman, who knows all about the medicines for childbirth. The things I learn from you about plant medicines I will write here in my book and share with the women of my land."

The bush women: "Well, maybe tomorrow we will tell you about the medicines, but tell us more about the women of your land."

This conversation would usually continue for a couple of hours, to the delight of the women. The women wanted to know such things as how many wives men have, whether we prefer one or more wives, whether the women of our land could plant cassava and paddle boats, how many children they have.

After a rapport had been established with the women, they would stroll casually by our tent and ask us to follow them into the jungle where they would search out plants used exclusively by women. They would give the local name for it and explain how and why it was used. We took samples of the plants and stored them for transport back to the Biological Laboratories at Harvard for analysis.

Mother-infant death during childbirth is rare but may occur when a woman cannot deliver the baby because the pelvic area is not large enough, the situation in which a caesarean might be performed. The midwife or medicine man would do their best to get the baby out, but if they were unsuccessful, the mother and infant would die and the entire village would mourn their passing. These bush people knew nothing of caesarean sections. In cases where the woman died in childbirth, it was said that a great *kunu* or curse had befallen the person and that she was by nature unfit to give birth. But in another part of the rain forest, we met a woman who

The Reunion

indicated that in rare cases where the fetus cannot come out normally, the *obeah* woman would remove it by a special technique not revealed to us.

We asked what other types of effects the *kunu* could have on the expectant mother and the child, and the women would describe cripples, distorted bodies, and other disabilities. One of these cases, a young boy of about twelve years with Down's syndrome, was assigned the task of putting a special red substance on the village hunting dogs in order to delouse them. This red substance, called *kaesoe,* is also used by the Indians to cover their dogs and cover their own bodies to repel parasites and bring healing spirits. The Afro-Americans probably learned the properties of this plant medicine from the Indians.

Why are some women cursed? They reply, "These things should not be discussed, but they usually descend on a person who is evil or dishonest." An evil person who has *yorica* (the devil) in him or her can put a strong curse on others, they said. If this curse is not removed by an *obeah* man, they may suffer very bad consequences such as losing a child, being hurt in the rapids, or being attacked by a jaguar. People accused of putting a *kunu* on others and accused of being a *wissimong* (sorcerer) reportedly have been brutally beaten by the victim's family. But people are not allowed to kill each other because of *kunu* curses.

What would a pregnant woman do if she knew that a *kunu* had been put on her? we asked. There were two recourses, the women answered. If it was late in the pregnancy, she would undergo an *obeah* ceremony to exorcise the evil spirit from the body. If the *kunu* were detected early in pregnancy, the woman would try to abort. Plants are used for abortion. The women showed us a plant called *ayoowiri* with yellow and red flowers and small hanging pods. The leaves and seeds of this plant are boiled in an infusion and taken orally to induce quick, uncomplicated abortion. The seeds of this plant are poisonous and cannot be ingested directly or whole.

We found a book in the library of the Swedish Royal Academy with a painting of the *ayoowiri* plant. This rare book, *Metamorphosis Insecterium Surinamensium*, which, it was said, had been opened only once by the king of Sweden in

The Reunion

1751 and once thereafter, was written by a white naturalist, Maria Sibylla Merian. A massive treatise, it describes in detail (including colorful drawings) some of the flora and fauna (mostly insects) of Surinam. On January 20, 1700, one of her entries deviated from her usually descriptive scientific protocol to reveal a rare moment of sisterhood with the local enslaved women:

This plant Flos Pavonis has seeds which are used by the slave women to induce abortion. The Indian slave women are very badly treated by their white enslavers and do not wish to bear children who must live under equally horrible conditions. The black slave women who are imported mainly from Guinea and Angola, also use this plant to prevent childbirth and seldom beget children. They often use this plant to commit suicide in the hope of returning to their native land through reincarnation, so that they may live in freedom with their loved ones while their bodies die here in slavery, as they have told me themselves.

This report stands in marked contrast to those published by certain Europeans and Americans today who claim to have evidence that "slaves were well treated and generally lived better than many white Americans of that period."

Opposite the text Merian painted a colorful portrait of the plant, with its bright red and yellow flowers and green pods. Several features of her *flos pavonis* were similar in detail to the *ayoowiri* that we had been shown by the bush women. It is the plant *flos pavonis* (flower of Pavon), known as *Caesalpiniae pulcherrimae* (named after the Italian botanist Andrea Cesalpino, with Latin for very beautiful). The scanty literature available on *C. pulcherrimae* describes it as a stimulating purgative that contains hydrocyanic acid, gallic acid, benzoic acid, and tanin; a dose of four grams will induce abortion in early pregnancy. We were able to trace this plant back to Angola, Togo, and other parts of West Africa where it grows abundantly and is used medicinally.

The plant's origin helps localize the areas from which the ancestors of today's Afro-Americans were stolen. It demonstrates that the enslaved Africans brought a knowledge of ethnopharmacology with them and were not entirely dependent on the indigenous Indians or their European captors for their knowledge of curative and other plants.

For the Living

Bush Afro-Americans believe very strongly in the supernatural. To them nothing—good or evil—merely happens; a spiritual power is always involved, and it is wise for everyone to be aware of it.

It is hard to remember when we first became aware of the bush dwellers' religious consciousness. It was probably when we first met our boatmen, all of whom were Bush Afro-Americans, and noticed the curious-looking amulets they all wore around their necks and wrists, some made of cowrie shells, some constructed from the rolled and plaited fibers of palm fronds, and others simply lengths of cord or string with decorative objects dangling from them. We sensed that there was something special, some purpose other than ornamentation, in these bracelets and necklaces.

The real significance of the amulets was demonstrated one day as our boat struggled through rapids, and one of the boatmen accidentally snapped his bracelet of cord and cowrie shells. The boatman threw up his hands signaling for us to stop the boat, shouting something that sounded like "*obie*." The other boatmen and our interpreter were as gravely concerned as was the panicked boatman, our interpreter explaining that it was a bad omen for the *obeah* to fall overboard. There was ample evidence that the boatman was badly affected by such a grave omen: he had to be restrained from leaping into the rapids in an attempt to retrieve his *obeah*.

Despite the general confusion, our guide remembered that something he had thought was a piece of a belt had flown loose and hit him on the side of the face, then dropped down between some stacks of equipment in the boat. "That was probably his *obeah*," said the guide, pointing at the boxes. The distraught boatman, excited at the thought that his *obeah* might not be lost after all, climbed over a stack of crates, looked in the area where the interpreter had pointed and found his *obeah*. He examined it fondly, uttered a brief prayer, and asked the other boatmen for some string to repair his bracelet.

We saw the weak-looking string that he was about to use, remembered the scene caused by the loss of an *obeah*, and tried to entice him into substituting a piece of nylon cord. He

The Reunion

Medicine man's
healing tools.

Typical small family
shrine, with bottle for
pouring libations.

Religious shrine with
skulls of bush cow.

Fertility shrine.

inspected the slender nylon and initially thought it inferior to his weak, old string, but a couple of aggressive test pulls on the nylon changed his mind.

Our trip continued. The river was quiet for a while and our interpreter told us about the significance of an *obeah*. It is believed to be a protective amulet, imbued with supernatural powers, made to each person's taste and specifications, and which inhibits physical and spiritual danger.

Before the boatmen ate or drank anything, they cast small bits of the food on the ground, poured out a few drops of their drink, and said a prayer, the musical, poetic, West African words "Nana Kadiamon Kadiampon" ("Father, the Unchanging One upon whom I lean and I will not fall"). The words seemed very familiar to us, and we realized that some of the lyrics and style of the spirituals that we know come from those who prayed to the same god in Africa. This respect by the bush people for a supreme deity was also observed by Captain John Stedman: "To what I have already advanced, I may add, that all negroes firmly believe the being of a *God*, upon whose goodness they rely, and whose power they adore, while they have no fear of death, and never taste food without offering a libation."

One day, traveling by river to the village of Samsisi, we noticed buzzards perched high in the giant trees. The scavengers took to the air and began circling overhead; there was a carcass somewhere below.

The boatman explained that buzzards, which they call *opete*, had been known in Africa before slavery and were kindly spirits. He said that *opete* had delivered some of the rebel ancestors out of the cruel slavery of the plantations to the safety and freedom of the jungle. The birds still have a religious significance among the bush people. "*Opete* is wise and sees all things." In Kumassi Ghana, one of the homelands of the bush dwellers' ancestors, the buzzard also has religious significance.

One evening we asked permission of the elders to visit the religious shrines in the village of Gado Saby. The village headman, Abahya, said that we could see some of the sacred shrines but that he had to accompany us. Some shrines are off limits to outsiders and most villagers. And there are sacred villages, like Dahomey; religious centers inhabited only by male and female priests. The natives boast that no

The Reunion

outsider has ever been permitted to enter Dahomey. The Surinam Ministry of Health has tried on several occasions to enter Dahomey and gather information about the health of the people; they thought there were sick and dying elderly people there. But Surinam's government officials were forbidden to enter the sacred village. We were asked by government officials to visit Dahomey and bring them information on the natives' health. The name Dahomey suggests that the village's first inhabitants probably were abducted from the West African country of the same name.

One shrine was a small house about five feet high constructed of neatly cut wood strips shaped with a machete. The roof was wooden and thatched. In front, there was a low-hanging gate where one entered kneeling. Inside was a wooden statue four feet high, which represented a white soldier. It had a helmet on its head, a thick moustache made of tiny wooden sticks, and a straight wiry beard of sticks. A spear was thrust through its heart. In front of this statue were sacred gourds in which libations were poured during prayers intended to "make the enemy weak and vulnerable in any attack against the village."

Another shrine, in the village of Maiki, is about seven feet high and is also made of wood and palm thatching. This shrine contains relics of the actual swords, spears, and eighteenth-century muskets that were used in the battles against the enslavers. Most were rusted and covered with the sacred *pemba dottee.* Inside, one of the medicine men was chanting a prayer and pouring a libation over the relics and an old stone on which the swords were sharpened during the revolutionary days. The prayer was a chant, praising the ancestors who defeated the enslavers and delivered them to freedom, beseeching the ancestors to continue to look over them and prevent outside forces from bringing destruction to their way of life.

The most majestic shrine was at a giant cottonwood tree whose base was surrounded by *azang paus.* This natural altar stood more than one hundred feet tall and had huge roots and a base that extended outward much like that of a cypress tree. The recessed area created at the base of this tree by the growth of the roots was like the shell of an amphitheater. The Bush Afro-Americans say that this cottonwood tree, which towers over the others in the forest, is the

The Reunion

Agheeda drummer calls villagers to worship.

Three villagers are washed with holy water by medicine man after marriage ceremony.

Wooden statue of
Dutch soldier made by
eighteenth-century
Afro-Americans during
the war periods.

One of the holiest of
ancestral veneration
shrines. It contains the
swords and muskets
used by the freedom
fighters.

Typical large shrine
where villagers come
to sit and pray.

dwelling place of certain spirits, and evil will befall anyone who harms it.

The special religious significance of this tree, called the *kon kon,* goes back to the time of their ancestors' arrival in Surinam. The high regard held for the *kon kon* tree was probably best expressed by a black slave more than two centuries ago, when Captain Stedman wrote;

Perceiving that it was their custom to bring their offerings to the wild cotton tree, I enquired of an old negro, why they paid such particular reverence and veneration to this growing piece of timber.

"This proceeds (said he) massera, from the following cause: having no churches nor places built for public worship (as you have) on the Coast of Guinea, and this tree being the largest and most beautiful growing there, our people, assembling under its branches when they are going to be instructed, are defended by it from the heavy rains and scorching sun. Under this tree our gadoman, or priest, delivers his lectures, and for this reason our common people have so much veneration for it, that they will not cut it down upon any account whatever,"

During a ritual ceremony at the tree, footsteps and the voice of a woman could be heard from behind the shrine in the direction of the neighboring village. Her voice grew louder as she approached the shrine, and attention strayed from the prayers and libation of the *obeah* man leading the ritual as people sought the source of the noises.

Suddenly a woman with a ghostly look appeared, her entire upper body daubed with white powdered clay *pemba dottee,* and her gaze would not settle on any in the crowd. With a spry but halting gait she circled the shrine, oblivious to the others, carrying a calabash gourd filled with *pemba dottee,* casting handfuls of the talcum-like clay in the direction of the *azang paus* which surrounded the cottonwood tree. All the while she chanted a religious song.

She completed her first circle around the shrine and cast some of the *pemba dottee* on the other people, somewhat startling them. But the *obeah* man was watching her and smiling with respect. He motioned for the other people to stand farther back from her path and just observe.

The woman circled the shrine three or four more times, and a multitude of voices, a chorus, came from the same direction as had the woman. Men, women, and children

Caesalpiniae pulcherrimae drawn by naturalist Maria Sybylla Merian on January 22, 1700.

C. pulcherrimae specimen from rain forest today.

Obeah woman
meditates before
sacred dance.

Obeah woman dances
at sacred shrine.

Large religious shrine with statue of a person and a cross. Villagers sometimes enter the gate for private worship.

Old *obeah* women stand guard over dead body in casket to keep evil spirits away.

Young man beats
apenti drum.

Typical hut in the
Aucaner and Aluku
(eastern) territories.

stood thirty yards from the tree shrine, back in the bush, singing. Their singing spurred the woman on, her movements changing from a majorette-like prance to a hopscotch, and she circled the tree incessantly, moving faster and faster. The relationship between her chants and those of the chorus was one of lead singer to background voices. The *obeah* man even joined in the chorus, although he stood apart from it, and their voices drove this woman into a frenzy, much like a southern black gospel choir where the lead soprano is inspired to such great vocal heights by the chorus that she becomes "happy" and starts "shouting."

A woman so full of the spiritual atmosphere of the shrine, the ceremony, and the chorus is said to have felt the *winti* spirit. The *winti* subject "speaks in tongues," much as the Sanctified people of the rural South do, and becomes oblivious to the surroundings.

This woman circled faster and faster, the call-and-response singing between her and the chorus growing louder and more emotional; she sang at a higher pitch than the chorus, her part becoming a wail. She looked and sounded like a soloist at a black funeral in the rural South who was chosen to sing not just because she was talented but because she knew the deceased, felt the pulse of the mourners, and could reach inside of those assembled and console them, easing their sense of loss. That was the case here; the woman was a widow still in mourning. This sweating, crying, singing woman with bloodshot eyes fixed in a gaze was in a state of rapture.

Her solo climaxed, the woman was beseiged by women from the chorus and the *obeah* man, who rushed to her side to congratulate her. Her body convulsed in jerking movements, she flailed her arms, and finally she came out of her trance. She didn't seem to know what had happened, but from the response of those around her she recognized that she had made quite an impression.

She took some of the *pemba dottee* from the *obeah* man's gourd and daubed all of the people with it, then danced in a circle and chanted a melodious "song of blessing." The *obeah* man gestured that the people kneel in prayer.

A most mysterious example of the religious practices of the bush people happened in the village of Gado Saby. Early one morning while all were still asleep in this remote village deep in the rain forest, the villagers were suddenly awakened by loud screams from one of the villagers, a pregnant woman running through the village from one side to the other. She stopped and vomited with a violent heave of what appeared to be blood for several minutes as she fell to her knees. The village had been awakened by the clamor but remained quiet, no one approaching the woman or even emerging from their huts. The screams gave way to crying and chanting, and moments later, the woman disappeared into her hut. There was silence in the village except for an occasional barking dog.

Half an hour later, about 6:00 A.M., the village began to stir, people going about their business as if nothing had happened. One of the elder villagers explained that a *kunu* had befallen this woman, and she feared that she and her child would suffer from this curse. The elder said that this woman had engaged in evil practices and that she had brought evil spirits on other villagers. The spiritual leaders of the village said that she had a large rat in her stomach along with the baby. The rat was said to be eating at the baby and trying to take its place. In the evening she would be given an exorcism to remove the rat by the *obeah* man in the presence of many of the adult villagers. Children were not allowed to participate or view the ritual.

Late in the day, an elder known as Kwasi walked into the bush to a clearing near the river. On the way he stopped at the hut of an older man named Akofay who handed Kwasi one of two beautifully carved wooden sticks, called *obeah tiki.* They waved the sticks and chanted a few words, performing a cleansing ritual of protection before the exorcism ceremony. They went into the woods, walking about a mile to an area where there were many small creeks or natural canals twenty to forty feet below a single log bridge. The area, completely hidden and treacherous, was difficult to reach. During the trek one of the men picked up a fast gait, unusual for Bush Afro-Americans, who do almost everything slowly and deliberately. The reason for the hasty gait was that the ground was teeming with large red ants. The bush men wore an herbal repellent and had callous soles on their feet several millimeters thick from going barefoot.

The Reunion

The area designated as the site of the ritual was a circular jungle clearing surrounded by dense foliage. Near the clearing were three huts partly covered by bush. In one hut was the dried skull of an animal that appeared to be a tapir, stuck on top of a pole. Other decorations on or near the hut indicated that the hut belonged to the *obeah* man. Forty villagers were assembled in the clearing. The drums began to beat and the women danced together, some of them chanting. The men, fewer in number, played drums or simply stood around clapping their hands.

From a thicket behind the *obeah* hut, a woman and a man walked out, escorting the pregnant woman who was to be exorcised. She was in tears, and laughing and crying as she chanted. The crowd parted, clearing a path for the entrance of the threesome. The woman was led around the entire semicircle of people for all to see. She fell to her knees and started vomiting as she had in the village that morning. There seemed to be blood in the vomit. She was taken to the center of the clearing and asked to lie flat on her back on some palm fronds. She lay there face up, looking terrified.

The Reunion

The villagers danced around her singing chants in unison for an hour, with brief interruptions for rest and the pouring of libations. By then, the pregnant woman, still lying on the ground, was soaked in perspiration. Occasionally she raised her hand to wipe her brow. On the signal of the *obeah* man, the women of the village came forward and spat upon her naked, pregnant stomach. Then both the women and men expectorated on her stomach until the *obeah* man signaled them to stop. The women rushed forward, leaned over her supine body, and rubbed the spit into her stomach. Medicinal liquid of leaves and herbs in water were sprinkled from calabash gourds all over her body from head to toe, amid moans and chants.

Without forewarning, and as if struck by lightning, the women kneeling around and all of the others jumped away from the pregnant woman, screaming frightfully. Some pointed their hands toward her, then quickly away from her body in a darting motion, as if following the direction of something moving fast. Some of the women clung to each other, yelling "rat." All claimed that they had seen a large rat leave her body and run off into the woods. And by their expressions it seemed that they believed they had seen something very frightening. We did not see the "rat" or anything else leave her body, but they were all convinced that they had seen it and were all talking about it excitedly, describing its length. The "exorcised" woman, who had stopped vomiting, was helped to her feet. She was smiling and embracing the women, and all the women and men hugged her and reassured her. She seemed ecstatic and appeared to be grateful to the villagers for their efforts in her behalf. The exorcised woman later walked through the village, talking amiably with her neighbors, and acting as if nothing had happened. She appeared healthy and carried out her daily chores. Later we learned that she gave birth to a normal, healthy girl.

For the Dead

No aspect of the bush religion is more heavily enshrouded in spiritualism than the phenomenon of death and the rituals that prepare the dead for burial and for the afterlife. These ceremonies are so elaborate that all kinds of mythologies have evolved about them. Myths are especially prevalent among the residents of coastal Surinam although few of these Westernized people have ever ventured into the deep bush. The spirits are believed to be especially strong in a village when someone dies. It is said that on one occasion a culprit at a funeral ritual was detected by the avenging spirit of the deceased turning his murderer's feet around backward.

Entering the village of Mainsee we knew that something was amiss: the people weren't as jovial as others had been in the villages where we had stopped farther downriver. The whole village seemed edgy. The headman dispensed with pleasantries and addressed the serious business of the hour. A woman of a very old and large clan had died; the spirits were stirring and the village was in deep mourning. In the conference house, the *krutu oso,* we were told that the villagers would be tense until the body was buried. Everyone in or near a village at the time of a death is suspected of wishing harm to the deceased, and this widespread suspicion often causes tempers to flare when someone begins to feel implicated. The woman had been dead for a few days. Her body had been cleansed and placed on a half section of a dugout canoe. It lay in state in the *dede oso* (funeral parlor) until the casket was constructed by a special guild of villagers. A watch is always kept near the casket in the *dede oso,* usually an *obeah* woman joined by a member of the family of the deceased.

When the casket, which looked like a small house, was completed, the woman's body was covered with the sacred *pemba dottee* and earthen clay and put into the casket with a few necessities for the afterlife. The top was sealed. The casket was placed in the *dede oso,* signaling that the dancing and drumming could begin that night. It would continue nightly until the body was taken away to be buried. The drumming progressed beyond the intermittent warm-up stage, and the singing and hand clapping grew louder. People standing in front of and facing the *dede oso* kept time with the drums, clapping their cupped hands. Young girls danced a few feet in front of the *dede oso,* facing the crowd. They clapped as they danced to the throbbing of the sweating drummers who sat to one side of the crowd.

The Reunion

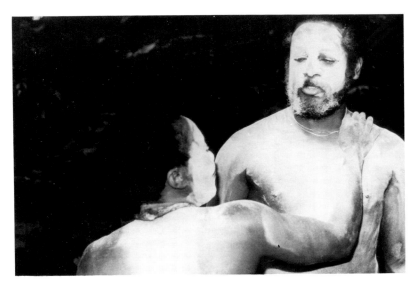

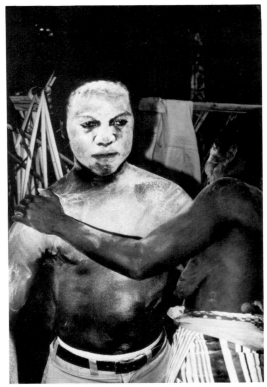

Obeah woman covers
Counter with sacred
powder.

Evans being covered
with sacred powder.

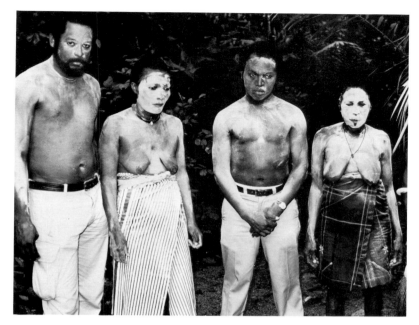

A second *obeah* woman joins the group.

Dancing *obeah* woman tosses sacred clay to bless Counter and Evans.

Many villagers danced that night, boys, girls, men and women, many of whom would dance again on subsequent nights. Most fascinating was the dance of a small albino man. He started very slowly, almost like a drunken man, out of step with the beat. It was easy to see, though, that his "missing the beat" was intentional and not from any lack of skill. As soon as he stepped onto the dance area in front of the *dede oso,* the crowd, especially the women, started to spur him on.

His dance was like that of a monkey or gorilla, and his pale skin and light eyes presented a marked contrast to the black faces in the crowd as he dipped, darted, and shook before the flickering bonfire. In a fevered pitch he rolled the front of his loincloth into a crude phallic symbol and by holding the lower parts of the tightly rolled loincloth tight between his thighs he made exaggerated pelvic thrusts. To the roars of the crowd and the upbeat drums, he thrusted and gyrated himself into exhaustion. He continued his dance, as did other villagers, at intervals for most of the night. There were fertility dances because birth is a major theme during a mourning period. It was curious to observe that the albino man, the one who was so clearly different, was the one to act the fool in the dance.

There was an unusual gathering down near the river early the next morning. The central figures were approximately a dozen men, all of them young and muscular, with pieces of cloth tied around their heads. The cloth looked like bandannas: in a knot across the forehead, hanging in a V-shape from the rear of the head down over the nape of the neck. After a brief period of drumming, the drums were put into boats, and the young men, armed with machetes, shotguns, and unusually large bundles of what appeared to be food, paddled away from the dock. They were the grave diggers, leaving to prepare the gravesite for the burial.

A small conference was taking place: the headman was talking to mourners from neighboring villages. Back in the village center, people were being ceremoniously washed. They kneeled before a man who poured liquid from a calabash over their heads while he whispered a prayer. Then they walked over to the *dede oso* where the casket rested like a house within a house.

The Reunion

Inside the *dede oso* an *obeah* woman sat, guarding the spirit of the dead, maintaining her vigil for most of the day, every day until the body was buried. She was spelled by a second *obeah* woman, so that the spiritual vigil could be maintained for twenty-four hours. No one entered the *dede oso* without the *obeah* woman's permission; to do so would be to disturb the spirit of the dead.

Suddenly there were shotgun blasts. It was a call-and-response sequence, the first muffled shot coming from a distance and answered by a responding shot only a hundred yards away. Villagers gathered at the river bank where the "response" shots had been fired. A flotilla of canoes appeared to be staging for an attack. There was drumming, an old trumpet was sounding, and the boats seemed to come together in a formation. The returning grave diggers were in the distance, their boats more elaborately decorated than they had been when they left. A crude mast and sail had been erected in one boat and a dead bird hung from it. The drumming and trumpeting grew louder as the procession, led by a canoe of relatives, neared the docking area.

The grave diggers hurriedly stepped ashore, some still carrying their machetes and shotguns and shouting and waving their hands wildly, and went directly to the *dede oso*. They removed the casket and put it on the ground in front of the hut. Testing its weight, the grave diggers lifted the casket and placed it on the heads of their two strongest fellows. One muscular young man was at the front of the casket and another at the rear. These two bearers approached some older men who were standing nearby, one of whom placed his hand on the casket just above the head of the front bearer and whispered. The bearers stepped away from the men but then approached them again. More whispering and more activity of the bearers; then they rocked the coffin side to side, retreated, and turned around in a circle. Suddenly the bearers stepped backward and ran off with the casket into another part of the village.

This little drama was a session where the spirit of the dead had been interrogated. The bearers were said to have gone into trances; through their movements the wishes of the spirit of the dead were carried out. Some of the questions the spirit asked were less serious than others—queries about

The Reunion

The funeral cortege.

the food supply for the mourners and the preparations. Others were more significant and concerned the progress of the grave digging. Still more serious inquiries made by the spirit of the deceased through the grave diggers were focused on anyone who had caused harm to the dead person while she lived or may have caused her death. When the bearers ran through the village, they believed the spirit was directing them toward suspects. They were taking the casket to the door of every hut and asking the spirit of the dead if people in the hut had wished evil on the deceased during her lifetime, a practice that keeps social pressure on the entire village to wish only good for their fellow people. Heated arguments and fistfights ensued when a person felt unfairly implicated. In the old days a person could be banished or killed if the spirit accused him of complicity in the death, but no such extreme responses are currently afforded the spirit of the dead.

There was excitement near the *dede oso;* the bearers were returning with the casket. They stopped in front of the *dede oso,* and there were more questions from the spirit of the dead, but the bearers did not run off this time. Four or five of the grave diggers lifted the casket from the heads of the bearers and set it on the ground. They lifted it up slightly off the ground two or three times, chanting a prayer, then put it back in the *dede oso.* The villagers wandered off in different directions.

It was dusk, and boats on the river were coming from all directions. Most of the people in the boats brought gifts of colorful cloth, food, or drink for the relatives and mourners. They would usually go first to the *krutu oso,* present their gifts, and be formally thanked.

There would be many visitors, numerous *krutus* about things natural and supernatural, nightly drumming, dancing, and singing at the *dede oso.* The goings and comings of the grave diggers would continue, as would the daily carrying of the casket with the spiritual interrogations, countless ritualistic washings, and the constant watch kept at the casket by the *obeah* woman, the relatives of the deceased, and the elders of the village.

On the final day, the grave diggers returned to the village with the same fanfare that had greeted their first arrival. There was a salute of exchanged shotgun blasts and drum-

The Reunion

Young grave diggers
carry old canoe on
which corpse has lain.

The grave diggers recite last prayers over the dead body before casket is removed to the burial site.

Grave diggers run with casket throughout village.

ming and trumpeting as the flotilla docked. This time, when the grave diggers went to the *dede oso,* they lifted up the half section of a canoe on which the body had lain before the casket was built. The canoe's half section was believed to contain the spirit of the dead, as did the casket. The two bearers carried it as they had the casket, and the interrogation and accusations were repeated. That night there would be more drumming, dancing, and singing. The crowd around the *dede oso* was larger, and the ceremony more intense.

The next morning there was more drumming and interrogation of the spirit as the casket was removed from the hut. Scores of villagers looked on, some waiting, as the casket was borne to the river and from there to the burial ground downriver in the jungle.

The Reunion

A Dugout and a House

Because the rivers represent the only thoroughfares in the bush a boat is an absolute necessity. Among the Bush-Afro-Americans, some of the first skills learned in the ways of the river are the construction and successful handling of a boat. The people are master boatmen and skilled craftsmen. Their boats are dugout canoes, but they are far superior to the crudely hewn-out floating logs often associated with so-called primitive people who use this form of water transportation. Their boats are works of art by any standard. The delicate balance that characterizes them seems to enhance their maneuverability. To this day they remain the only boats that are able to withstand repeated collisions with the rocks in the rapids and hold together.

The boats are built by many people in a village, and they reflect certain idiosyncrasies, but there is some general uniformity. They normally range in length from twenty-two to twenty-five feet, or from forty-four to forty-eight feet. Larger boats sometimes have modified sterns to accommodate outboard motors. The motorized boats are primarily used by boatmen who work as supply haulers for the Surinam government, handymen for missionaries, or transporters of timber downriver.

The first stage of building a boat is the search for the proper tree. When Moti, a villager, headed into the bush in search of a specimen, he and his fellow woodsmen carried only their machetes and a single-bit axe. They kept a quick pace until they came to a tree set back from the path. They started toward it, using their machetes to clear the way. Hacking away some of the bramble near the base of the tree, Moti put his ear close to the trunk and struck the tree with the back of his axe. There were a few seconds of silence, and he hit it again. He smiled and signaled to his friends that this was a good tree. They all began chopping away the small growth near the base of the tree.

While the two other villagers continued to clear the underbrush, Moti and his fellow woodsmen began cutting down some long, straight trees only five or six inches in diameter. They cut the leaves and branches from these saplings and made ten-foot long forked sticks out of three of them. They stripped others of leaves and branches and cut them into poles about twelve feet long. They were preparing the platform from which they could cut down the tree. Using some

The Reunion

twigs and a small tree limb that he pushed into the ground, Moti built a miniature platform around the limb, explaining that, like the miniature, the big platform would surround the tree and stand about eight feet above ground. The axemen need to be where the trunk of the tree is of a uniform diameter, so that the tree will be less difficult to prepare and drag to the river bank. More important, the cut tree will be easier to shape into a boat.

By now the two axemen had driven the ten-foot-long forked sticks into the ground. Each was placed about three to four feet away from the trunk of the tree and about 120 degrees apart as one walked around the tree. They tied the other three straight poles, end to end, into the forked tops of the poles they had driven into the ground. The ends of these poles were secured with vines. Finally there was a triangular platform around the tree that did look very much like the miniature one. The axemen climbed up on the platform, and Moti positioned himself in one corner of the triangle while his mate braced himself in another corner. One man had to cut left-handed and the other right-handed. Both men had to balance their feet on the small green poles and at the same time swing mightily to cut down this giant tree. Before they started their cutting, the axemen hesitated, and one of the two men on the ground prayed, saying that the tree was being taken for good purpose.

Three hours after the cutting began, the huge tree cracked and started to fall. The men on the platform yelled as they threw down their axes, swung down from the poles, and ran from the falling giant. When the dust had settled, there was a massive clearing, a swath, that had been cut when the tree fell. The spirits of the woods were thanked, limbs were cut from the trunk, and the sixty-foot log was left to season from ten days to two months. Later it would be dragged to the river bank and shaped into a boat.

The stages of boat building can take up to a month depending on the boatwright(s). The skilled craftsman works on a long cocoonlike shell and a log stripped of its bark. The cocoon was the freshly hewn shell of a boat now ready for the burning and stretching stages. The other was a log that was only one stage beyond the tree that the woodsmen had cut in the forest.

The Reunion

226

Old tools used by the
natives in making
boats.

Shaping a new dugout
with a hand axe.

Another "boat" looked somewhat like a cocoon but had been opened and was surrounded by stakes tied together. The stakes were driven securely into the ground at intervals along either side of the shell directly across from each other. The tops of the stakes extended a few inches above the boat and rested against its sides. Stakes directly across from each other were tightly bound together with vines, thus creating a vice that prevented the shell from opening too much during the drying process. Inside the shell was evidence of recent burning. Inside and at intervals along the length of the boat were criss-crossed sticks (stays) to keep the shell, opened during the burning, from closing as it dried. There the stays would remain until the boat hardened into form.

We walked back to where a man had been stripping the bark from the log with an axe and machete. He had begun to shave or level off the top side of the log with his axe as he prepared the log for hollowing.

By late in the day he had hewn out a significant part of the log. The tool that he was using was an adz with a handle that must have been eighteen inches long, and it resembled a miniature hoe. A smaller adz lay nearby. Once the hollowing got down to a point where a bad swing or chop of the longer-handled adz could permanently damage the shell, the smaller one was used. The final hollowing on the inside of the shell must be done carefully because an errant blow or dig of the adz can weaken the shell and cause it to crack during the burning and stretching. The outside of the shell must be made smooth and uniform too because humps and other irregularities in thickness create extreme stress points on the shell during the stretching and crack the boat. To avoid outside nonuniformities, the craftsman moves along the shell feeling for discontinuities with the fingertips of his left hand, hacking or shaving them away with his small axe.

It was our luck to learn that a boat in a village across the river would be burned and stretched the next day. Early the next morning, the boatmakers had already begun their work. The shell was placed upon a platform that consisted of two short cross-poles (at either end of the shell) that held it a couple of feet above the ground. A fire had already been started inside the shell, and a man was putting more dry leaves into the fire. The outside of the middle section of the shell seemed to have been smeared with mud. The fire grew

The Reunion

larger, and finally one of the boatwrights picked up a bucket and threw water on the fire. The burning was going too fast and had to be slowed down. Periodically another man would approach the boat with some wet leaves and stroke the outer sides in the area of the burning to keep moisture in the wood. After fifteen minutes, the boat was flipped over on the platform and the burning was allowed to continue underneath for another twenty-five minutes. The boat was taken down from the platform and the stretching began.

Using their hands and long sticks with forked tips, they began at one end to pull the shell open before it dried. This was done with great care to avoid cracking. As soon as the shell was opened to the desired width, the criss-crossed stays were inserted. The men moved progressively along the length of the boat, pulling it open and inserting the stays. One boatwright, down on his knees observing the opening of the shell very closely, shouted, *"Topoo, topoo!"* He pointed at a spot on the outside of the shell that he thought might crack. The stretching was stopped; he picked up his axe and started to shave away some wood in the area of the spot. A couple of minutes later the stretching continued until there were criss-crossed stays all along the inside of the boat.

The stakes were brought out, the boat was moved a few feet over, and they were driven into the ground all along the outside of the boat. They were all tightly bound and the boat was weighted down and put into a "vise." It would remain there for a week.

When the boat is removed from the vise, the benches and end-pieces are installed. They serve two purposes: they are seats, but they also serve as stress members to keep the boat from warping. Some of the boats have long boards attached to each side, running the entire length of the boat. They are sawed from logs, carved, and shaved to fit the boat to which they are attached. According to individual taste, the stems and sterns are decorated with pieces of metal received from outsiders. Some of the boats are beautifully painted, others are left natural, depending on the tribe or nation constructing the boat. The tree ritualistically taken from the forest is now a boat, indeed a work of art, ready to transport these ancient and traditional people up and down the rivers.

The Reunion

Evans examines
boatmakers' work.

Testing an unfinished
boat in rough waters.

Young boy rides stern
of well-balanced
Saramaccan dugout.

231

Teaching young boy to use *kulu* stick in rapids.

Children race in long
dugout.

Evans tests a new
family dugout.

An old man paddles
through rough rapids.

Mother and daughter
in typical Aucaner
boat.

The bush dwellers' hut is equally as beautiful and is the product of boards sawed from the tree trunks and woven palm fronds. It is impossible to ignore the beautiful wood paneling that makes up the front part of the huts. The hand-carved finishings in the front paneling and on the door are exquisitely worked and tempting to touch. The traditional dirt-floor huts are made primarily of wood and woven palm fronds.

The frame and siding are made of wood, and the front and back can be either wood or woven palm fronds, but the roof of the traditional house is always made of overbush laid panels of the tightly woven palm fronds. The bush people are skilled at braiding the leaves and tying them together, and a roof constructed from them is rainproof.

The frame of a hut is built by first installing four wooden posts in the ground at an approximate depth of three feet. The posts are located at the four corners of a rectangle about ten feet by twenty feet. They are connected at their bases by some heavy pieces of timber that are hewn from small trees. The three-foot depth and the heavy wooden connections between the posts make for a solid and stable foundation.

The siding is made of boards that are crudely sawed from logs with a two-man hand saw. These sideboards are attached to the posts, one above the other, up to the top of the posts about four and a half feet above the ground. If the front and back are to be made of wood, the boards are attached the same way, except a space is left in the front wall for the door.

The roof is gabled, but the eaves are exaggerated and reach almost down to the ground on either side. This extension of the roof is to protect the sides of the house from the direct rays of the sun and to make the inside somewhat cooler. The roof also extends out from the front of the house to shade the front door and protect against rain.

In the front and rear on the inside of the frame are two king posts installed to support the ridgepole. The ends of the long rafters are tied together in pairs along the ridgepole with vines. The other ends extend down across the special grooves cut into the top sideboard of the frame and reach almost to the ground. When the panels of tightly woven

The Reunion

Frame of hut.

Men cover one side of
hut's frame with palm
fronds.

Covering opposite side
with palm fronds,
working from bottom
to top.

Young man directs
construction of the hut.

Finishing off top of
hut.

palm fronds are laid horizontally along the rafters, the exaggerated eaves are created.

The weaving of the palm fronds is more tedious and slow than the actual assembly of the house. Once an adequate supply of palm branches is prepared and a group of villagers gather, the roof can go up in short order.

It is in the front of the house, especially a wooden-front house, that the artistic idiosyncrasies of the owner are best expressed. Some use paint; others use a hand-carved mixture of naturally finished woods. Still others use a combination of painting and carving. Unlike the building of the house, which is routine, the decoration of the front wall is a long, creative project and can take months.

Before the front wall was installed for the villager Kwasi, we watched a small ceremony. Kwasi's brother-in-law (one of the helpers) joined him, his wife, and baby in the front beneath the extended roof, and poured a libation asking God's blessings on the house and "all who dwell therein."

Later a partition of woven palm fronds would be installed inside the house to separate it into two rooms, the front room for sitting and eating, the back room for communal sleeping. The parents and older children sleep in hammocks, small children on padded surfaces.

The floor is kept from flooding during rain by digging trenches around the huts to drain off the water. It is an effective method. The huts do not flood during even the hardest rain.

The traditional hut with its beautifully woven roof has sustained the Bush Afro-Americans for three centuries, but it is slowly giving way to the corrugated metal roof. Only in the most remote parts of the interior of Surinam is there no sign of this creeping change. This metal roof can alter the ambient temperature and heat flow of a thatched hut significantly, in some cases causing body sores to its inhabitants. But a corrugated roof does not need to be replaced as often as a natural one and is sold to the bush people by outsiders as an advancement that requires less maintenance and is more protective.

The Reunion

Typical house in the
Saramacca (central)
territory of Surinam.

Typical Aucaner house.
The woman living in
this hut has many
suitors, represented by
the number of paddles
over her door.

Red, Black, in Green

Some of the men of the village of Saniki were planning a journey to trade at Indian villages along the Brazilian border and we decided to join them. One evening before we left, there was a meeting at the hut of Quacoo to choose the leader of the group. Only a few men would make the journey, and they would travel in three large boats. Their barter and trade exchanges were for themselves as well as other members of the village who could not make the trip. Some of the men wanted bows and arrows brought back, others wanted hunting dogs, still others wanted baskets and various items for the women. Such trading has been going on for over three hundred years, since the time of the first meeting between the Bush Afro-Americans and the aboriginal Indians in the New World.

The Afro-Americans are especially fond of the hunting dogs that the Indians breed and train to hunt specific kinds of animals. A dog can be trained to hunt tapirs only, or small deer or the wild pig. The origin of these dogs is unknown, but they bear a striking resemblance to the small dogs seen in West Africa. Possibly the dogs did originate in Africa and were brought to South America by the Portuguese slavers who sold them to the coastal Indians, who in turn traded them to inland Bush Indians.

Quacoo, six men, and three small boys would make the journey to the Indian villages in a few days. The entire journey would take about seven or eight days: three days to go there, three days to return, and two days of trading. It is known that the Bush Indians are not very receptive to outsiders. One old man even warned the men not to touch anything in the Indian village; the Indians had "lots of poisons lying around which could kill upon touch."

On the day of departure the travelers to the *Inge Conde* (Indian lands) assembled at the river at about 7:00 A.M. Many of the villagers came to see us off, some with large machetes (a favorite item to trade with the Indians), others with domestic chickens in wooden cages. Some had turtles, tobacco, and cloth. The items to be traded were loaded into the boats, and we all got in and took our seats. The crowd on the shore bid us farewell as we moved the large forty-foot canoe into the river and pushed away.

One man stood at the front of the boat with the long *kulu* stick to guide us through the rocks. Two other boats contain-

The Reunion

ing four men each followed by several meters. One small boy sat in each boat. The boys were being taken along by their uncles to observe and learn how to trade with the Indians.

Traveling upstream in turbulent water for several hours, the boat dropped suddenly several feet and we seemed to be going downhill. The men yelled and struggled to steady the boat. They had just gone over some large rocks and a six-foot cascade. The rocks seemed to get larger and the river more difficult to negotiate as they progressed upstream, but by then they were accustomed to the tough water. The current seemed much stronger and the noise of the rushing water much louder. Beyond the overhanging foliage and just beyond us were magnificent waterfalls. They were large, wide, and colorful, with a misty rainbow over them. Occasionally a fish jumped up near us. We could not get the boat through the waterfalls and had to cross on foot.

The boatmen began to guide the boat toward the shoreline, careful not to turn over in the swells and lose the goods. When they reached shore, everyone got out of the boats and helped pull them onto the shore. Several small logs were put under the boats to serve as rollers, making sliding the boats across land much easier. On land the boats were pushed and pulled through small but well-traveled paths in the forest around the cataracts. The men knew this trail very well. They had followed it to Indian territory for many years.

After about two hours of struggle they were around the large cascades, and the boats were put back in the water. After a brief rest and food, we continued upstream. The going was even tougher this time. There were more rocks in the water, and some of the swells seemed impassable. Rains came and beat harder by the hours. If we hit a small waterfall too quickly, the boat would drop four or five feet. Another large cascade lay just ahead. Like the last one, this one was massive and could be heard roaring in the distance. Again the boats were aimed toward shore; the boatmen got out and carried them overland through small paths running alongside the waterfalls. Things moved faster this time; the boatmen were hurrying because there was one more cascade to pass before nightfall. The rivers are too treacherous

The Reunion

to travel by night, especially with all of the trade goods. On their way for a second time, there were a few hours of paddling and singing before we reached the third waterfall. By the time we crossed this one, it was nightfall and we pitched camp.

The next morning we got started about 6:00 A.M., traveling many miles and passing several large and small waterfalls, much like the first day. On the third day we were still moving upriver toward the Indian villages. One of the boatmen was concerned that there had not been any Indians on the river. Usually, he said, there was a vigil all along the rivers of their territory to watch for outsiders.

At about 2:00 P.M. on the third day, an older, experienced boatman ordered the paddlers to slow down and move quietly up a small tributary off the river on the right. As we turned, we could see people moving in the distance. The old boatman again warned them to go slowly, and they continued to paddle up the quiet river tributary toward the Indian villages.

The figures began to take the forms of real people as they neared. There were an old man, two old women, three young women, and some small children, all washing themselves or working in the river. The old man was working on a fish trap, and the women were cleaning and eviscerating some animals. The children were splashing and playing in the water. When they saw the boatmen, they all stopped and stared. One of the boatmen turned around and noticed boats behind his: three small canoes with two Indians each in them. Each canoe had followed them for the last quarter of a mile, one watching each boat, to protect their villagers from outsiders. Each Indian wore only a red loincloth and had long dark hair, shiny with oil. Each had a long bow at his side.

The oldest boatman went ashore first and greeted the old Indian man. They embraced each other like old friends and started a friendly conversation. The other Indian men now came alongside the boats and waited while the old men talked. Then some of the other boatmen struck up conversations with the younger Indian men in the boats, who by now were inspecting the goods brought to trade. The Indian men wore only loincloths with monkey-hair belts. Some had black

The Reunion

Counter and Evans
traveling to Indian
village to witness
trading practices.

paint on their faces. The boatmen were waved to shore by the head boatman, who started up a hill to the village known as Apoti. Most of the Indian men were about five feet, four inches tall, but a few were as tall as six feet. The women wore only loincloths. Most were short and stout, withdrawn, and ostensibly timid. The scenes came right out of the pages of Stedman's drawings of the 1700s. One Indian woman of about thirty was standing in the path as we traveled toward the village. She had an infant wrapped in a cloth and hung around her shoulders and a small child at her feet.

As we entered the village, the dogs started barking. Some were vicious enough to make the boatmen scamper about, and that was a source of laughter among the children. But the bush people are not fearful of dog bites. One bushman who was severely bitten on his hand by a hunting dog simply went to the river and washed away the blood, then put some earth on it and patted it with a stick until the bleeding stopped. He went about his work as if nothing had happened.

The huts in the Indian villages were different from those in Afro-American villages. The Indian huts' structure is circular rather than rectangular and, except for the poles holding them up, were made entirely of straw and palm leaves. They were higher from floor to ceiling inside and had numerous hammocks hanging from large poles about four feet above the ground.

As we reached the center of the village, a second elderly Indian emerged from his hut to greet us. He embraced the head boatman and called him by his first name. Other villagers came forward and greeted us cheerfully. This elderly Indian, named Seetee, was the headman of the village. He called for a *krutu,* a term that comes from the Bush Afro-American language. The two groups took turns speaking each other's language as a matter of courtesy; the Africans spoke the Indian language, Tolono, and the Indians spoke the Bush Afro-American tongue.

There are several Indian tribes in this area: the Wayana, Trio, and Akurio among them. Most of them have decided to live in one region to protect themselves from the encroachment of outsiders. Many call themselves the Tolono people, after the Tolono River in that area.

The Reunion

The *krutu* said that this village and those surrounding it had few occupants—only about ninety men, women, and children. Most of the tribespeople had migrated many days upstream to villages on the Tolono River, leaving only a few behind who would follow them later. Some of the villages around Apoti had been damaged by heavy rains, and much of the food supply and wild game had been depleted. The Afro-Americans were disappointed. They had come a great distance.

The Bush Indians and Afro-Americans made arrangements to trade for some of the things in the village, including dogs, even though the scale of the trading was not what the Afro-Americans had hoped for. The eighty miles to the new Indian villages upstream were too far for the party to travel, so they decided to spend several nights in the Indian village and head back to Saniki a few days later with the few items that had been available for trade. Just after the *krutu,* the young Afro-American boys were off hunting with the Indian boys. They used both slingshots and bow and arrow to shoot birds and *agouti.*

The Indians were shy but friendly and warm. They had a strong affection for the Bush Afro-Americans whom they referred to as Mekōlō, which means a human like the black ant. The Indians believe that God fashioned people as he had ants, some brown, some black, some white—all "children of the same Great Spirit" but with different colors. The Indians are called Tolono, the brown ant.

Their name for the white man is *panikētē*, which they say means "one who will kill his friends." As whites entered the bush, the Indians went deeper into the interior to hide because the "*panikētē* would take their children and kill them." Like the Bush Afro-Americans, these people retain oral history memories of the savage slaughter and enslavement of their people by Spanish, Portuguese, Dutch, English, French, and German adventurers. They said that "such behavior was natural in the *panikētē*" and that "it could not be changed in them." Even today the women tell the children to stay clear of the *panikētē* and to run and warn the village if one is spotted. As recently as the late 1970s, a group of Indians told a white missionary that they had plotted to kill him until, after several months' observation, they decided he would not bring harm to their children.

The Reunion

Counter and Evans
participate in *krutu* in
Indian village.

Dogs traded by the
Indians.

The actual trade (or
barter) negotiations.

Stedman's drawing
of the same tribe two
centuries ago.

Typical Tolono
("Amerindian") woman
with two children.

Counter shares food
with young Indian
mother.

For years, U.S. historians, anthropologists, and other interested groups have pondered the relationship between the Afro-Americans and Indians who came in contact with each other for the first time in the New World. Their meeting may be called a historical accident. Some of the Euro-American history books tell us that the Indians, who were viewed by the Euro-Americans as unprofitable slaves (they violently resisted, and died readily when held captive), were used to track escaped slaves. Other historical sources tell us that black slaves occasionally escaped to sovereign Indian territory where they were adopted by the tribe and integrated into the culture, some becoming chieftains.

Tribal stories and songs tell two sides of the same legendary event: the first contact between the Afro-Americans and the so-called American Indians, centuries ago. Neither group recognized the other as inhabitants of a strange and far-off continent. The Indians thought the blacks were "a heretofore unseen Indian nation." (Even today, the vast Amazon region hides tribes of Indians who differ markedly in complexion and who have seldom been seen by other tribes.) And the Afro-Americans thought that they were still in Africa and mistook the Indians for Africans of a distant region.

The Bush Afro-Americans repeated for the Indians the story of how they escaped the *bakrah-panikētē* and were confused as they groped in the deceptively familiar rain forest for the "road back home." Indians rescued them, fed them, and guided them to the safety of Afro-American villages then springing up in the jungle interior. The Indians sometimes led black fugitives for hundreds of miles, eluding European troops and hired slave catchers. When European soldiers invaded the bush to recapture black fugitives who regarded themselves as escaped prisoners of war, Indians fought side by side with blacks, using poisoned spears, darts, and arrows. They often spread out to warn blacks of the approach of pursuing white soldiers. Blacks would live in Indian villages for months, even years, until they were able to resettle in safe Afro-American villages. Many grew so attached to their rescuers that they spoke of themselves as *"Inge bloka"* or Indian blacks.

The solidarity among the newly arrived Africans and Indians is illustrated in a seventeenth-century document in the Algemeen Rijks Archive in the Hague. It is a report to the

The Reunion

Processing the manioc cassava root.

governor of Surinam from a Colonel Cruetz, who had been sent to meet with the Bush Afro-American chieftain, Adu, to obtain a peace treaty. One condition was that the Africans should reveal the whereabouts of the Indian tribesmen who helped them in their successful struggles for freedom. Chief Adu refused. "You have come to make peace with us," he told Cruetz, "and the Indians should not concern you. They are our brothers and we will never reveal to you the location of their villages."

The Indians' principal spokesman was Chief Atepa, a statuesque and articulate leader of the Tolono tribe. He and other leaders explained that their forebears were apprehensive of the blacks at first, largely because of their goods and weapons. Wooden boats, machetes, and other metal weapons and tools were unknown to some of the Indian tribes. Their fears were allayed; Mekolo proved not only peaceful but generous with their possessions. They taught some of the Indian nations (who shaped boats from papyrus) how to burn, stretch, and carve the wood of a single tree to make a dugout canoe. They introduced the Indians to the use of tools and other relatively sophisticated implements.

In return, the Indians shared their knowledge of hunting, agriculture, and medicine. They instructed the blacks in the use of curare and a chemical they call *manamee,* used in hunting tree animals like monkeys. This plant is lethal, and only selected adults are permitted to see it processed. They

The Reunion

wear leaf masks covering their noses and mouths so as not to breathe the fumes. When *manamee* is put on the tip of an arrow and shot into a large tree monkey, it induces violent convulsions, causing the monkey to become limp and fall from the tree to the ground. When the monkey has fallen, the hunter cuts out the skin and muscle around the arrow mark to remove the excess poison. If *manamee* is not used in a monkey hunt, the injured animal would lock its prehensile tail around the tree tops and die. Manamee acts like strychnine, causing massive excitation of spinal nerves by releasing all of the nervous system's inhibition.

Like the bush women, the Indian women are very knowledgeable about plant medicines. Knowledge of these medicines was shared with the Mekolo women two centuries ago and continues to be shared. The Indian women also shared their knowledge of food preparation and agriculture with the early Afro-American women.

The blacks told the Indians about some of their medicines, like *singafu* (*costus spiralis*), the gingerlike plant that cures certain stomach ailments, and *ampuku,* which is used to heal broken bones, and others they had used in Africa. It is well documented that the early and latter-day Bush Afro-Americans convinced the Indians to trade with them exclusively and not with *panikētē,* whom they said were anthropophagi who would eat the Indians.

The first formal agreements between the blacks and Indians involved sharing and using land. A barter agreement (*mati*), still in operation, evolved. The blacks would raid coastal plantations and Dutch military stations for useful equipment; some of it was to be traded to the Indians for hammocks, woven baskets, bows and arrows, corn, and hunting dogs.

In our many talk sessions with the Tolono leaders, we learned that their ancestors were impressed by the powerful physical stature of the Mekolo. They said they had never seen men and women so broad-chested and muscular. The blacks were the fiercest, most valiant fighters they had ever encountered. With few guns and limited ammunition they had defeated entire European battalions. The Indians were awed that Mekolo men and women continued to repel attackers even after parts of their bodies were blown off by muskets.

The Reunion

Woman carries large
cake of cassava bread.

Woman prepares to
wash domesticated
pig.

255

Large monkeys shot by
arrow with a tip poison
called *manamee.*

A cooked monkey's
head hung up to keep
away evil spirits.

Woman prepares
monkeys for cooking
and eating.

Special medical tests on Indian villager.

Boatman with Indian friend and family.

Bush and Indian men
are delighted to see
each other.

Indian man points
direction for Bush
Afro-American.

Observing the trading.

Young Indian boy
found after wandering
in dense rain forest for
two years.

Counter helps Indian friend get the feel of a 70-pound American-made hunting bow.

Two young women in boat help to escort Counter and Evans down river as part of the departure ceremonies.

The Indians also admired the Mekolo women for their fighting and hunting prowess and for their service in the leadership of the village hierarchy. The Indians saw that the black women could be equal to the men in military combat and began teaching hunting and fighting skills to some of the women of their own tribes.

Bush Afro-Americans and Indians live in neighboring but separate villages. Members of different tribes sometimes hunt or fish together or share food. The Afro-Americans are sometimes called upon to help settle disputes among Indian tribal groups. Intermarriage is rare. Both tribes say their young are free to marry across racial lines but that their ways of life are so dissimilar that few would consider doing so. The Africans, they pointed out, are river dwellers; most of the Indian tribes are bush dwellers who live deeper in the rain forest.

Monkey meat, prepared by the women, is roasted after the monkey has been skinned, eviscerated, and all of its teeth removed. Beautiful necklaces are made with monkey teeth, and the hair is woven into belts for the men's loincloths. The meat is roasted thoroughly over fire and eaten when it is fairly well done. The taste is not unlike that of pork. The head of the monkey is usually smoked and kept in the hut to ward off Yawahoo, the Indian name for the devil.

The outside world became aware of the stone age tribe called the Akurio in 1968 when Christian-converted Indian tribesmen were sent out to the rain forest on the Brazilian border to wander and locate other Indians for conversion. The Akurios had never left the dense jungle canopy and indeed had never had much exposure to sunlight. Their skin is much lighter than that of other Indians.

They did not know how to make fire when they were found, yet they had fire in their camps. They indicated that their tribe had simply forgotten how to make fire for many generations, if, indeed it had ever known. When they moved from one campsite to another on their nomadic trips throughout the vast northern Amazon, they carried the hot coals from the previous campsite to the new village in hollowed tree stumps. Sentries were posted at the old campsite to guard the burning coals until a reliable fire could be started at the new camp. They said that this had been going on for many generations, hundred of years, and they were

The Reunion

"always afraid that the fires would go out," meaning an end to their people.

Today some of the Akurios live with the Tolono people, but others have returned to the jungles on the Brazilian border because they feel that life in the Indian village is "too noisy." By our standards these villages are absolutely quiet, but the Akurios have reference to the noise of dogs and other domestic animals, which they did not have in their comparatively quiet jungle setting.

We went into the hunting grounds with the Akurios and watched them hunt with spears and bows. They were magnificently skilled hunters. Their favorite food is honey, and they will climb even the tallest tree to collect it. (Falling from tall trees was their major cause of accidental death, we were told.) When they found that we had several small jars of honey, they would visit our tent frequently to ask for it, sometimes to trade their beautiful combs and monkey-tooth necklaces for it.

The Indian population we studied seemed to be free of serious hearing impairment, even though they, like the black bush dwellers, eat cassava bread.

We have seen many changes among them in our subsequent visits to their villages. Missionaries have begun to reach more of them. Beneath their tribal lands, like those of the Bush Afro-Americans, lie rich lodes of bauxite, gold, and other minerals, and the inevitable encroachment of extractive industry is displacing them and their game animals. And recently white Rhodesians have been emigrating and resettling in nearby Amazon areas and given large plots of Indian land for "development."

The Reunion

The Future

For three centuries the Bush Afro-Americans have been a nation within a nation. They have remained independent and faithful to African traditions like no other group in the New World. But now their independence is threatened as it never was before. This threat is not from the force of arms, as was the one so bravely repelled by their ancestors during the hundred-year struggle of the seventeenth and eighteenth centuries. It is the exhaustion of many of their natural resources combined with the expansion of Western civilization into areas that once isolated and protected them from outside influences. They are losing control of their lives and their livelihood.

There have always been attempts from outsiders to influence the lives of the Bush Afro-Americans. Following the peace treaties of the eighteenth century, this influence was thwarted by the bush dwellers themselves. For example, limits were set on the number of Bush Afro-Americans who could visit coastal towns at any one time. Later, through the establishment of the position of postholder (a kind of ambassador from the capital) among the people in the peripheral bush, as well as the efforts of missionaries, attempts were made to "civilize," proselytize, and educate the Bush Afro-Americans. These efforts met with little success because they were based on the notion that the "paganisms" and "idol worship" of the Bush Afro-Americans were worthless.

Also there has been a long-standing interest among certain Surinam groups in cultivating the vast rain forest area of the country, and the natural labor force to do this, it is believed, is the bush people. Not only would they be making a positive contribution to the greater society of the country but, in developing the interior and becoming less isolated, it would be easier for the state to integrate them, according to these groups.

The Bush Afro-Americans are losing the fight against modern influences. This was evident in the villages on the river where some of the women were cooking in aluminum pots and pans. These signs of the slow encroachment of the outside world were not nearly as profound as a phenomenon that we observed as we traveled upriver, stopping occasionally in villages. We were puzzled by a near total absence of young men and teenage boys. We thought that they might have been in the woods clearing the fields, but this was the

The Reunion

harvest season and the women did the harvesting. We were even more confused as we traveled deeper into the bush and noticed that the presence of young men gradually increased as the villages became more remote.

An elder told us that the missing young men had gone downriver to work in the mining industries, were working on the river as transporters for the Surinam government or as general purpose boatmen, or were working in the cities of St. Laurent, Cayenne, or Paramaribo. In villages located within two or three days' travel from the coast, the game had become scarce and much of the good farming area had been exhausted. "Sometimes a man hunts for days at a time and only kills a couple of birds," he said. Because of this, he said some of his people had to go downriver to find work to support themselves and their families. The work usually involved such backbreaking tasks as clearing segments of land in the rain forest, digging up the earth, or hauling supplies on the river. The tough physical requirements of the work were such that the *bakrah* seldom, if ever, hired an older man and never a crippled or a visibly sick man. Sometimes this work kept the men away from the villages for months at a time. He said that some of the younger unmarried boys never came back, and, if they did, it was only for a visit and they often brought "bad habits" back with them. "Many of them have lost respect for the elders and for our way of life. Maybe it is good that they don't come back."

The elder opposed this type of uncontrolled travel downriver to work for *bakrah,* but as an afterthought he said "a man has to eat." He went on to say, "In the old days only those who were confident in the ways of the bush were allowed to go downriver to trade with *bakrah.* They knew that our way was superior to those on the coast and they came back."

When asked why the tribes had not withdrawn farther into the bush, he said that some of them had, but it was not easy. They are organized into extended families and clans that can date back to the first escapes from the plantations. These clans are assigned plots of land, and to move to better hunting and planting grounds means moving a great distance from one's family. "Nonetheless," he said, "some of them have moved on and it is only a matter of a few months or a few years before the things of *bakrah* reach them."

The Reunion

In his youth he had helped to float logs downriver and did not believe that all of the "things of *bakrah* were bad. Gesturing toward his hut he said, "My shotgun and my axe are *bakrah* things." Reminiscing, he said that in the old days there was more control over what a person could bring back. The useless playthings of the *bakrah* were forbidden.

Asked why he had not followed his proud brethren upriver, he responded, "My heart goes with them but somebody must remain to teach the young boys about the spirits, the ways of the river, to hunt, to make boats, to build a house, to carve and to play the *agheeda* and *apenti* drums."

During one of our later visits to a village on the Surinam river, deep in the rain forest, a younger man of thirty-five said that his attitude was not that of an isolationist. He had worked downriver for an American mining company and had returned to live with his people. When he first returned and began trying to convince the elders that the day of isolation from the modern world was over, he was assailed as a *bakrah nange* (white man's negro). He even proposed to cut an airstrip out of the jungle so that small planes could land, hoping to open his village to some of the conveniences of the outside world. He was attacked for his notions and once was hacked at with a machete. He showed us scars from the machete and said that he had argued in *krutu* after *krutu* with the elders. "I was trying to convince them that *lanti* [the Surinam government] was prepared to help us by sending needed supplies and an occasional medical doctor. I told them that *lanti* was more likely to do this if the trip into the bush was a two-hour airplane flight instead of a ten-day boat trip." He said that he was finally allowed to cut the airstrip, although some of his people moved as far away from it as they could in an attempt to "stay away from *bakrah*." The ones who stayed warned him that if the airstrip brought evil to the village, the spirits would kill him. "They told me that I would die a slow and painful death with sores all over me if I brought harm into this land," he said. He said that he was not afraid because he, too, "knew the *obeah*" and would be protected; in his heart he believed he was doing what was right for his people.

As he spoke, we heard the distant roar of an airplane engine, the plane that had been sent to fetch us. It was a moment of great contrast for us to see this man in loincloth

The Reunion

with white chalk all over his face and body, telling us of his readiness for modernization and his respect for tradition, as the twin-engine plane touched down on his newly cut airstrip. He, like many other of his people, had one foot in the modern Western world but was holding tenaciously to three-hundred-year-old traditions.

In subsequent visits to Surinam we saw evidence of a great many changes in the bush country and the attitudes of the government. More and more of the Bush Afro-Americans and Indians were being displaced by industrial ventures. Many extractive industries were encroaching on their lands. Change was sweeping over many of their villages. In one area, what had been beautifully thatched grass huts the year before were now small wooden shacks with tin roofs, some provided by the industries or the government. Some of the younger bush Afro-Americans viewed this change as progress and accepted it, while others felt that their culture was being destroyed and were struggling against change in order to salvage their culture. We were certain that these people, like their proud ancestors, would flee farther into the bush. But we knew that, sadly, in a few years there would be little left of this culture. We have been fortunate to be allowed to step back in time and see what our ancestors were truly like. Their survival is living proof that you can break the back, you can break the heart, but you cannot break the spirit of a people determined to be free.

Our departure from the bush country of Surinam was marked by deep sadness for us and many of the people we had come to know as friends and family. On the eve of our departure, we visited many of our friends to thank them for their hospitality and bid them farewell. The people seemed deeply saddened by our departure, and asked us to return soon. Some even suggested we come and live with them in the bush. It was a moving time for us, but we knew that we had to leave and return to our homes and jobs.

On the night before our departure, we were feted by the entire village of Sanniki. Wild pigs, three *agoutis*, and large fish were roasted over a large open pit fire. The entire night was filled with drumming, dancing, and singing. The songs of the early evening were sad, but as the night wore on and the spirits became lighter, they became more joyful.

The Reunion

A young friend waves
goodbye.

Young woman bids
Evans farewell.

The villagers escort
Counter and Evans
down river.

The villagers brought us many gifts: beautiful boat paddles, wood-carved calabash dishes, food paddles, and peanut pounding boards. The young women brought us fruit for our journey back home. We danced and sang and played music on a tape recorder until early the next morning. We slept only three hours, then were up with the sun. The village was already alive with the people busily going about their daily chores. With the help of our boatmen, we packed our gear and prepared to leave this beautiful bush nation.

When we made one last visit to bid farewell to the chieftains and *bahjahs*, many wished us well. Embracing us, the chieftains invited us to "come back to the rivers and live with the bush people." We promised to return soon.

Scores of villagers waited at their boats to escort us back downstream. The holy man then came, dramatically blessing the water, and asking it carry us away safely and bring us back again. Two young girls who earlier had helped guide us to the nearby villages had prepared their boat for us and wanted us to ride the first couple of miles to the rough waters with them. We joined them and headed downstream. A multitude of boats followed us; we could not count them. The people sang a stirring song as they paddled, which said, essentially, "Goodby, Kwame Samu, goodbye Kwaku Dabe (the African names they had given us). We know you will come again."

When we reached the big rock in the river, about three miles from the village, we moved alongside our large dugout canoes and stepped into them. We waved a last goodbye and headed back to the outside world.

The Reunion

Epilogue

We returned to Harvard and set about processing our films and other recorded material. During that time we conducted an informal poll around the university, finding that, except for a few social scientists, no one was aware of the existence of the Bush Afro-Americans. Several months later we had prepared a series of lecture materials on our scientific and cultural findings.

Our first program about the Bush Afro-Americans was held at the Harvard Radcliffe Afro-American Cultural Center early in 1972 for Harvard students and faculty. The reception was overwhelmingly positive, and the question-and-answer period following the presentation was longer than the presentation itself. The most common reaction was, "Why have we never heard of these people and their successful struggle against slavery?" In answer, we explained that a few books had been written in this century about the bush people of Surinam, but they had not been written from an Afro-American perspective and had not gained widespread recognition or acceptance among blacks.

Following this initial presentation, we were beseiged with requests for lectures and film programs. Students and staff of all ethnic backgrounds came to the lectures and were as enthusiastic about this story as were Afro-Americans. In fact, we received almost as many requests for the presentation of our lecture from white and Asian students as from blacks.

Interest in this topic spread to other universities in the Boston area, then throughout Massachusetts and to other New England schools. Over the next few years we presented the film-lecture show all over the world: Meharry Medical College, Tennessee State University, Fisk University, Howard University, Washington University, University of California, Berkeley, UCLA, Purdue University, Rollins College, Abilene Christian College, Dyess Air Force Base, Karolinska Nobel Institute (Sweden), Peking University, and Nanking University, to name a few.

In the spring of 1974 we appeared on national television in a one-hour special. This show, called "The Original Brother," was produced by television producer Tony Brown, and the national response to the show was enthusiastic. We received scores of letters of inquiry and congratulations, especially from Afro-Americans, which inspired us to broaden our research and film efforts.

After more visits in 1974 and 1975 to the rain forests, we produced a one-hour film documentary, which summarized our years of getting to know bush people. We named this film after the famous historical village, Boo Coo, which means "I shall moulder before I shall be taken."

We wanted a trained narrator who could convey the power and emotion that the images in our film evoked and were fortunate to meet actor James Earl Jones, who became deeply interested in the subject and eventually agreed to narrate the film. We could feel his enjoyment and involvement as he worked. "These scenes have the sound and look of Africa, but your ears and eyes deceive you— Africa is not where you are." Jones gave us a masterpiece of narration, which enhanced the quality of the documentary immeasurably.

A banquet in honor of the film premiere was held at Harvard in June 1976. Presidents Derek Bok and Matina Horner of Harvard and Radcliffe were our hosts. The second "premiere" of our film was held in the deep Surinam rain forest. Using drum communication and messengers, the chieftains sent word out to other nearby villages that Kwaku Dabe and Kwame Samu had returned with a special gift for all of the bush people. Using a portable electrical generator, a film projector, a long extension cord, and for a screen a large white sheet hung on the side of a hut, we created a makeshift movie theater in the center of the village. The villagers came from miles around, bringing their infants, their young children, and even their dogs. They placed their *bangis* in a semicircle about thirty to forty yards from the screen and waited quietly, both nervous and excited.

We told them that there was nothing to fear from the images they were about to see and tried to explain how film works, but when we asked them to come closer to the screen, they politely refused, holding their ground about thirty or so yards away from it. We decided that if we went ahead and showed the film anyway, their fears might well diminish as their curiosity grew.

When the film began to roll, a profound silence fell over the group. The first scenes showed the medicine man, Apauti, whose face and entire body had been painted with white clay. The people watched intensely as the medicine man danced about in the sacred gyrations so familiar to them. Then, villagers whom they all recognized appeared, and they saw themselves on the screen. We began to see occasional smiles of recognition. As always, it was the children who broke the ice, laughing, even cheering when they saw friends and family members appear in the film. The children moved closer and closer to the screen, finally touching it, and hollering loudly when they recognized their friends in the film. Young adults and teenagers began laughing at the youngsters' reaction and moved in closer to the screen. When the sacred Kromanti dance

Epilogue

began in the film, Apauti, the medicine man and spiritual leader of the bush people, entranced by the film, leapt into the air and started dancing, as if captured by the filmed ritual. Afterward he was embarrassed, saying he was sorry but he could not help himself. At the end of the film, many of the villagers were touching the screen, pointing to people they knew, and cheering. They asked us to show it again, and again.

The first-time viewers quickly became enthusiastic critics of the editing process, saying, "You cannot go from the village of Sanniki to the village of Pokaytay in a jump; it takes hours," or "How can you look at Apauti's entire body and then run up on his face and look in his eyes so quickly? This is trickery; something is not right." Things that we took for granted, like switching scenes from one setting to some distant setting or zooming the camera in on a person's face after viewing his whole body, were startling to them.

Late in the summer of 1976, President Ferrier of the Republic of Surinam sponsored the Paramaribo premiere of our film, with the entire Surinam government and hundreds of other guests in the audience. President Ferrier said that the film "was the best record he had ever seen of the culture of the bush people," that it "would be used in the schools to teach the history of the 'Bush Negroes,' and kept in the government's archives as the official record of the bush people." Later in a letter sent to us at Harvard, he stated, "I . . . considered the film an excellent representation of the still-existing elements of the cultural heritage of our Bush Negroes. . . . This film will help to preserve the knowledge of these elements for future generations."

We were encouraged to take our film to a national television audience and negotiated a prime-time airing on the Public Broadcasting System, the only network that agreed not to change the content or context of our film. PBS decided that to ensure a much wider audience, we would have to obtain a nationally known figure to serve as host. The Surinam story itself made the final decision about that.

Earlier in 1976 we had met the author of a book that was just then beginning to become popular. The author was Alex Haley, and his book was *Roots*. He had praised our work and had just completed the search for *his* African ancestry. We had been searching for the connecting link between Africa and all Afro-Americans. It could be said that we had found the "Kunta Kintes" who managed to escape slavery. In many ways the Bush Afro-Americans of Surinam represent the living proof of the people Haley so accurately described in *Roots*.

The live characters in our film conjured up images of some of the proud Africans and Afro-Americans about whom Haley had written. One very touching similarity was that one of Haley's characters was

Epilogue

A large photograph of the statue stolen in the 1800s is returned to the village (presented at film premiere).

Counter and Evans with James Earl Jones.

On the set of Tony Brown's Journal, the authors' first TV appearance.

Alex Haley joins Counter and Evans on television set of "I Sought My Brother."

named Pompey, a name frequently given to newly acquired slaves by their enslavers. We had met a sixty-year-old Bush Afro-American by the name of Pompey who had never ventured out of the deep bush and who told us that he was a direct descendant of an escaped slave. He said that the name had been passed down in his clan for many generations.

We called the program, "I Sought My Brother," from a poem that we had both heard in church during our youth: "I sought my friend and my friend forsook me; I sought my God and my God eluded me. I sought my brother and found all three."

The film was shown nationwide on the Public Broadcasting System in April 1978, and the program received favorable reviews in many major national publications, including the *Pittsburgh Courier, Boston Globe, Washington Post,* and *New York Times.* The film has now been shown throughout the world, including the People's Republic of China, Japan, Kuwait, Saudi Arabia, Ghana, Brazil, England, France, and Sweden.

In response to our lecture tour and our film, the one question we have been asked repeatedly is, "Have you written anything on your work in Surinam?" That question prompted this book.

We hope that this pictorial essay has given readers the experience of stepping back in time with us, visiting the only blacks in this hemisphere who have remained so close to the African ways of their ancestors who first stepped off the slave ships some three hundred years ago. The Bush Afro-Americans represent one of the finest chapters in our history; they are the true blood and soul of all Afro-Americans. They show us that our ancestors were an independent, proud, and dignified people.

Epilogue